Art and Science of Law Instruction

Daily Messages Journaling
A Law Faculty's Year

Nelson P. Miller

Art and science of law instruction: daily messages journaling a law faculty's year.

Miller, Nelson P.

Published by:

Crown Management LLC – August 2020

1527 Pineridge Drive
Grand Haven, MI 49417
USA

ISBN-13: 978-1-63625-799-0

For law professors who treasure their craft.

Table of Contents

Introduction

This book collects a year's worth of daily, early morning messages to law professors teaching at multiple campuses in different regions of the country. The purpose for the daily messages was certainly not to direct how to teach law, nor to reform or correct ongoing instruction. The law professors receiving the daily messages were all accomplished lawyers and educators, perfectly fit for their academic profession, just as for their law profession. They could ignore the messages, as many of them surely did in their busy days filled with more-pressing communications and tasks.

Rather, these messages were to capture and share in collegial voice what the community of law professors were exploring as enhancements to their teaching craft. We read and hear of the value of journaling, recording what we are doing to examine how we can enjoy and enrich it, perhaps doing it better. In that sense, these messages were an exercise in collective journaling. If few of us have time to reflect and write, then perhaps one or a few of us can reflect and write for the rest. These daily messages serve as a collective journal.

These daily messages confirm that teaching and learning involve community. No law professor is an island. The classroom, whether in person or virtual, to the professor feels isolating, lonely. Yet students circulate merrily from class to class, dissolving that isolation into one big, rich broth to which each professor adds meat, spice, or vegetable. No professor should be exactly like any other. Indeed, no professor should be exactly like that professor was the prior term or will be the next term. This journal of daily messages shows the depth and breadth of a law faculty as a community of passionate learners.

The book's two parts, beginning with one-hundred-sixty messages on classroom instruction followed by seventy-four messages on online instruction, are the product of happenstance rather than plan. The virus crisis intervened to move all instruction at the law school to online remote learning. That move augured that the daily messages support professors in meeting the challenges of online rather than classroom instruction. The two forums have many similarities but several stark differences. The two parts obviously overlap in their content and application but also have messages that apply only to their own forum.

The book does not include the many attachments and links that went along with the messages. Those attachments and links are available to anyone who asks. The attachments and links are by far the more-valuable resource than this journal, especially when they are to studies, books, articles, and other writings by experts in the field of teaching and learning. The messages' author professes zero expertise, just an insatiable appetite for investigating and applying the expertise of others—like any other lawyer. Let's hope this collection, though, reminds us of the depth and breadth of those expert resources.

Part I

Classroom Instruction

Enhancing Classroom Instruction No. 1: Introduction

[Morale] [08/07/19]
Good morning colleagues, those thirty-six of you who are teaching MBE-tested required courses in the Fall. Thank you for the confidence you showed yesterday in sharing with me this journey of exploring ways to do better what we've been doing well together for so long. President McGrath will be guiding me in beginning this renewed effort, but first this thank you and acknowledgement of your service and expertise.

Every term, we climb the same mountain. The students with whom we climb differ every term, but we always start again at the bottom with students who are new to the climb. And we always reach the top, although with stragglers and a few lost. Any effort to improve the climb, to find new routes that bring more students to the top with greater skill and energy, must first be cautious not to lose sight of the summit nor how we've gotten so many so surely to the top. You are indubitably a skilled and committed, even intrepid, group. We have learned much together already. Your affirmation yesterday shows that you believe we can together nonetheless find a few surer, swifter routes up. Just please do not take any initiative, effort, offer, or communication as lacking appreciation for the skills you already richly possess in helping students do what they must do, which is make that steady climb to the top.

Let's each continue to be the joyful, earnest, insightful guide who we are, even as we explore together how to do so with even greater skill. And so we learn, rule by rule, precept by precept. Enjoy the day, and enjoy the coming renewed journey up the mountain. More soon to come. As you've probably guessed, I've been maniacally organizing, reorganizing, drafting, and otherwise preparing resources and offerings with house-afire urgency since James' first mention of the possibility. [Smile emoji.]
Nelson

Enhancing Classroom Instruction No. 2: Flashcards
[Resources] [08/08/19]
Good morning, trusted colleagues. Here's a quick note about the controversial flashcard issue. Whatever we think of them, they probably have a place, and to some students, a foundational place. Some of the

school's strongest graduates have used them heavily to pass the bar without commercial-course help, while they can give struggling students a working familiarity with precise use of weekly key concepts.

But to be effective, they need proper design and use. Commercial flashcards can be little more than outlines stuffed on tiny cards. To be effective, a flashcard needs a brief prompt on one side and a still-relatively short memory aid (the law concept to memorize) on the other side, like the attached cards for your Fall MBE-tested course or courses. Students can use them alone or, better yet, in pairs, one briefly prompting the other while turning the card back and forth on the least error or delay until the reciting students quickly learns card after card. Using a working deck of three to five cards and shuffling newer and older cards in and out of the working deck prompts new learning with old retrieval for those beneficial spaced-repetition and interleaving effects.

The attached cards for your Fall MBE-tested course or courses help students learn all MBE topics within your course—not everything you'll help them learn, but all topics off the MBE outline for your course. If you list them as a course resource, then the bookstore will print them for you and provide them to students for around $5. Please consider sharing them. The WMU grad-student team urges that we make them a core component of active learning. If you devote as little as five minutes in class to them in pairs, then you may be amazed at the explosion of intense retrieval rehearsal that you will witness, every one of your students speaking law precisely and repeatedly. Remarkable. Hope you find it useful, and please let me know if you are already using a similar resource.

Nelson

P.S. If I'd had your syllabus, then I'd have put tiny numbers down in the corner of the cards to indicate the weeks, for easier initial use and more-effective shuffling. But the grad team tells us that any marks or colors on the cards reduce their efficacy by creating false-association supporting stimuli, so the numbers are a questionable convenience. Interesting.

Enhancing Classroom Instruction No. 3: Research Abstracts
[Research] [08/09/19]
Good morning, MBE-tested-course professors. Here's a quick tip about a new learning-research resource.

President McGrath's presentations on teaching and learning highlighted several books summarizing recent research, the results of which challenge myths about learning. The library has ordered those books for any of us to read.

If finding the time to read the full texts challenges you unduly, then you can read my abstracts of those texts in a shared file that I will be sharing with you as soon as more of the texts arrive. In the meantime, I attach a first abstract of President McGrath's recommended book *How We Learn*. If the abstracts are still too dense to translate into ready action, then I have a Quick Tips file started to share with you soon, a cursory review of which may give you some ready inspiration for specific enhancements.

Look soon for both the full Abstracts file and those Quick Tips, accepting the attached single abstract in the meantime. And please feel free to send me your own research-study recommendations for abstracting and sharing. Good, science-based work is out there for us to find and mine. Enjoy the weekend.
Nelson
P.S. Okay, I snuck a second abstract into the attached file on the value of print over digital text for reflective and analytic learning. Couldn't resist.

Enhancing Classroom Instruction No. 4: In-Class Exercises
[Resources] [08/12/19]
Good morning, MBE-tested-course professors. This message attaches for your use or inspiration eight sample in-class exercises with answers for the MBE-tested course or courses you are teaching this Fall.

If enhancing instruction entails greater engagement in class, especially around instructional exercises that speed frequent precise practice with instant feedback, then we need to discern, locate or create, and implement those designs.

The attached eight sample designs for each of your courses vary just enough in their format to help develop slightly different skills, not just precise recall but also issue spotting, elaboration, distinguishing, application, and even problem solving.

Students working in pairs in class can steam through these exercises in just five to ten minutes each, meaning that students may complete several of these exercises in any one class session without overly reducing lecture, discussion, and recitation.

If you find these exercises helpful, then feel free to create more like them on other topics in your course or courses, or ask me to help you do so. You can tell from the flashcards already offered my interest in helping with content as much as design.

Nelson

P.S. Other available designs offer review, role plays, drafting, and other activities. The attached exercises focus on learning, applying, and analyzing law.

Enhancing Classroom Instruction No. 5: MBE Topics

[Resources] [08/13/19]

Good morning, MBE-tested-course professors. Attached for your reference are the MBE topics for your Fall course or courses, together with long-form and short-form outlines for those topics.

We each teach many things outside of MBE topics, especially practical things but also Michigan, Florida, or other-state distinctions and other topics that we know are important to practice in our fields.

Still, knowing what the MBE tests can help us align our instruction and assessment to the exam on which nearly all graduates of the school expecting a law license must do reasonably well. I hope these resources help. Enjoy the week.

Nelson

Enhancing Classroom Instruction No. 6: MBE Multiple-Choice Questions

[Resources] [08/14/19]

Good morning, MBE-tested-course professors. Attached for your use, if you've not already seen them, are multiple-choice questions on each of the MBE-tested topics in your Fall course or courses, keyed to the National Conference of Bar Examiners' MBE-topics list.

Please make whatever use of these questions you wish. The school already shares them as bar-exam resources. I use the questions as patterns for new exam questions and the keyed topics list to be sure that I am distributing questions evenly.

Thank you for your interest, and enjoy the rest of the week.
Nelson

Enhancing Classroom Instruction No. 7: Course Folders
[Resources] [08/15/19]
Good morning, MBE-course professors. Please accept a quick note on organization. You've received emails the last couple of weeks with attached flashcards, long and short outlines, and multiple-choice questions for each of your MBE-tested courses.

To help you keep track of those and other resources, you are about to receive a link to a shared folder titled as your Fall MBE-tested course or courses. That shared folder contains all the resources that you've already received by email, in some cases with a few other resources. I can also add other resources as you and your colleagues develop or wish to share them.

While you will find that shared folder by either following the email's link or in your "Shared with Me" folder, you can also move (copy) that shared folder over into your own "My Drive" folder to make it easier for you to locate. Please let me know if you have any questions or problems finding shared folders or resources.
Nelson

Enhancing Classroom Instruction No. 8: Student Advising
[Resources] [08/16/19]
Good morning, MBE-course professors. Here at this link is a quick offer of a slightly different resource or set of resources. Beginning Tuesday, after a brief survey on resources, I hope to share with you some videos on methods, having concluded initial sharing of resources.

Here is a brief explanation of what is available at the link. While we focus on enhancing instruction, we retain our responsibility to advise students on curriculum, careers, job opportunities, and other professional issues. You may find yourself giving rushed advice on any one or more of those subjects.

To speed and enhance your advising, while possibly relieving some of the time that it takes, this link is to a Student Books folder that contains free books on these advising subjects: Navigating the Curriculum; Choosing a Career; Getting a Job; Lawyer Finances; Cross-Cultural Service; Being Entrepreneurial; Bar Prep; Faithful Lawyers; MBE 400 Questions; MBE 700 Questions; and MBE Outline.

Please feel free to share these pdf files of books with students, placing the books on your Canvas page if you wish. They are all available on Amazon in print, but the pdf files are free and convenient for tablets or computers. I hope they help.
Nelson

Enhancing Classroom Instruction No. 9: Drafting Help
[Resources] [08/19/19]
Good morning, MBE-tested-course professors. You have already received sample exercises for the MBE-tested course or courses you will teach this Fall, which are also in the course folder shared with you. Please take sixty seconds to answer this survey about your interest in more in-class exercises for your MBE-tested courses this Fall. Thank you!
Nelson

Enhancing Classroom Instruction No. 10: Aligning to the MBE
[Methods] [08/20/19]
Good morning, MBE-tested-course professors. This three-minute video, which you can make a 90-second video by using the Settings icon to play it in double time, urges aligning instruction to the Multistate Bar Exam and explains how the shared resources are so aligned. I hope it helps. Enjoy the day.
Nelson

Enhancing Classroom Instruction No. 11: Introducing Engagement
[Methods] [08/21/19]
Good morning, MBE-tested-course professors. Here is a six-minute video (speed it up using the Settings icon) on how to introduce, structure, and supervise in-class engagement for maximum beneficial effect.

While we routinely lose the outside-of-class study battle to jobs, families, and other student responsibilities, we can win through in-class engagement.

Implement in-class exercises that reward students who study much outside of class but also serve students who study little outside of class. This video may help. Enjoy the day.
Nelson

Enhancing Classroom Instruction No. 12: Doing Over Telling
[Methods] [08/22/19]
Good morning, MBE-tested-course professors. Here's another three-minute video, this one on the advantages of getting students to do what you want them to do, over telling them what to do.

We all face the frustration of students not doing what we tell them to do. Our frustration, though, does not fulfill our responsibility. We should instead engineer ways other than telling, to get students doing.

Consider using a portion of class time for doing over telling. Take the one most-critical activity in which you want students to engage, and do it in the classroom, in a dynamic environment with instant feedback. And enjoy the day.
Nelson

Enhancing Classroom Instruction No. 13: Measuring Success
[Assessment] [08/23/19]
Good morning, MBE-tested-course professors. You've just received a link to a video advocating that your course-average grade over your course-average predicted grade is a sound measure of your instruction's effectiveness. Here, to help you evaluate your effectiveness at the end of the term, is the predicted average grade for your course or courses this coming term:

Torts II (TB): 2.65

The question is how much better than prediction can we do? A gain of a tenth of a grade point would be small. A gain of two or three tenths over

the predicted grades would be better. A gain of half a grade over predicted would be a strong showing. What will it take to make that gain? If we all make strong gains, then bar results should improve dramatically. Go for it. Here to help.
Nelson

Enhancing Classroom Instruction No. 14: Choosing Exercises
[Methods] [08/26/19]
Good morning, MBE-tested-course professors. This email shares a link to a short video on what in-class exercises to choose when considering how to increase in-class engagement.

Increasing in-class engagement is a sound strategy, but like any strategy, its success depends on how we implement it. Engagement should concentrate around topic-relevant, high-repetition, instant-feedback exercises.

Properly designed flashcards, properly used, can be a foundation but would only be a foundation. Exercises in issue spotting (where the memorized rules apply), application (how to deploy the rules in those settings), and analysis (how to structure application) should ideally follow.

Other videos this week will address more specifics on how to effectively increase in-class engagement, holding due attention of all learners, without waste of time. Enjoy the week.
Nelson

Enhancing Classroom Instruction No. 15: Using Flashcards
[Methods] [08/27/19]
Good morning, MBE-tested-course professors. This email shares a link to a short video on how students may best use flashcards. The method is just as important as the resource, and the video gives some tips on that method.

The point of flashcards is to produce instant, accurate recall (fluent recall) on presentation of a brief trigger or prompt. Staring at the prompt side of a card while pausing, mumbling, or paraphrasing inaccurate recall isn't the method.

11

The student presenting the card should just immediately flip the card to the recall side for the working student to repeat the recall quickly and accurately out loud. This method is faster and more accurate, and builds fluent recall.

The method also involves a working deck of three to five cards for the student to master, and then slipping additional cards into the deck while slowly dropping out the mastered cards. Encourage students to use proper method. And enjoy the week.
Nelson

Enhancing Classroom Instruction No. 16: Tracking Fluency
[Methods] [08/28/19]
Good morning, MBE-tested-course professors. This email includes a link to a short video on how students can track their fluent (prompt and accurate) recall of key concepts in your course or courses.

We know that what gets counted gets attention. When you help students chart, day to day and week to week, how fast and accurate their recall is of concepts you identify as critical, you give them incentive to work more diligently.

I am sharing with you separately the Fluency Tracker template that you can offer any student or all students in your class. The template shows the actual results (easily deleted) for one student who especially appreciated the tool. Enjoy the rest of the week.
Nelson

Enhancing Classroom Instruction No. 17: Best Exercises
[Methods] [08/29/19]
Good morning, MBE-tested-course professors. This email links to a short video on the best in-class exercises, comparing and contrasting several exercises to suggest which have the highest value for frequent, focused practice with instant feedback.

Sometimes (often? always?!), we don't have the time in class to accomplish all that we would wish. More significantly, students also face time constraints. Using high-frequency, focused practice can help students maximize the value of limited time.

As always, I hope you find something of value in this video. Enjoy the last of the week.
Nelson

Enhancing Classroom Instruction No. 18: Staging Exercises
[Methods] [08/30/19]
Good morning, MBE-tested-course professors. This email shares a link to a short video on how to introduce in-class exercises and move from one exercise to another for best structure and consistent full engagement.

During group activities, classes can easily devolve into unguided, study-hall-like discussion, unless we have clear structure engaging students and set firm expectations for participation. Exercises should also build on one another.

The video available through this link suggests ways to structure exercises to maintain consistent full engagement around the most-valuable exercises. I hope you find something helpful here. Enjoy the holiday weekend.
Nelson

Enhancing Classroom Instruction No. 19: Frequent Assessment
[Assessment] [09/03/19]
Good morning, MBE-tested-course professors. This email, on the first joyous day of the new term, links to a video on the value of frequent assessment, a subject with which we are all familiar but that bears keeping in mind.

We know the data showing that a single final examination forms a procrastination curve that retards recall and frustrates learning. We also know the data that frequent interim assessment fosters a testing effect that preserves recall and maximizes overall effort.

WMU collaborator Dr. Doug Johnson's first recommendation to us years ago was to institute five equal-weight (20%) graded assessments throughout the term, to defeat the procrastination curve and take

advantage of the testing effect. Let's keep moving toward the best use of assessment. Enjoy the new term.
Nelson

Enhancing Classroom Instruction No. 20: Assessment Rubrics
[Methods] [09/04/19]
Good morning, MBE-tested-course professors. This email shares a link to a short video on how to use an electronic assessment rubric to speed, objectify, and increase the detail and structure of your essay-exam feedback.

How swiftly, surely, finely, and reliably we can produce individual feedback for students throughout the term goes a long way to determining how effective our instruction will be.

You can get feedback on a well-designed assessment rubric into the email inbox of several students before an interim exam is done, a few more before the class ends, and the rest in the hours or day after the exam, a 24-hour turn-around.

I am sending access to a Templates folder that includes the fluency tracker already sent to you and the assessment rubric to which this video refers. I hope you find something here helpful. Enjoy the rest of the week.
Nelson

Enhancing Classroom Instruction No. 21: Recommendations Folder
[Methods] [09/05/19]
Good morning, MBE-tested-course professors. This email shares a link to a folder of the eleven videos sent to you over the past couple of weeks. The folder shares a handful of other resources explained in messages over the next few days. But with yesterday's last of eleven consecutive videos, you might want them here all in one place.

By the way, at President McGrath's behest, our collaborator WMU Instructional-Design Lab director Dr. Doug Johnson is taking a greater role, attending law classes this term in Kalamazoo to be able to give more direction not only to us but to his grad-student team members working with us. At his request, I present tomorrow to WMU Provost Jen

Bott and the WMU Psychology Department on our collaboration's success over the last six years.

Thank you for your interest, and more to come.
Nelson

Enhancing Classroom Instruction No. 22: Make It Stick
[Research] [09/06/19]
Good morning, MBE-tested-course professors. Attached for your interest is an abstract of President McGrath's recommended book *Make It Stick: The Science of Successful Learning.*

The psychology-researcher and journalist authors document in well-organized and highly readable fashion major myths that instructors and students believe about learning, contrary to growing evidence.

You are familiar with several of the insights about things like the value of retrieval practice, the laudable testing effect, and spacing and interleaving studies and recall. Read the book or abstract for reminders of these important concepts.

You may not be so familiar with the authors' other insights like the powerfully negative effect of the illusion of knowing, how unhelpful learning-style theory can be, and the plasticity of intelligence auguring a growth mindset.

The authors end with a chapter on practical applications that should inspire you to experiment with various enhancements to your instruction. The goal? Make it stick, meaning to make learning persist, which defines learning, doesn't it? Enjoy.
Nelson

Enhancing Classroom Instruction No. 23: Quick Tips
[Research] [09/09/19]
Good morning, MBE-tested-course professors. This email shares a file of quick tips drawn from the books that President McGrath and others have recommended, abstracts of which you have been receiving recently.

You may find hard, turning book or even abstract insights into practical classroom applications. What do you actually do, and where does the reading and research all end? The quick-tips file available through this link turns insight into application.

More abstracts are coming. With each abstract, you will find additional quick tips in this shared file. Enjoy the week and emerging new term.
Nelson

Enhancing Classroom Instruction No. 24: Other Schools
[Research] [09/10/19]
Good morning, MBE-tested-course professors. Please accept this analysis of an article in the just-published edition of the National Conference of Bar Examiner's quarterly publication, about the strategies that five law schools employed to improve their bar-exam results.

If you've been following the bar-exam challenge, you might guess the five schools: FIU, UMass, UNH, UNC, and Utah. In this publication, each school wrote their own three-page summary of what they've done. Each did something different. None did exactly what we have done to improve results, but one came close.

The publication illustrates one thing: bar-exam success doesn't offer a single approach. Indeed, each summary more or less said so. Each law school did what they thought was best. Importantly, we will not succeed doing what others did, while others would not succeed doing what we have done and will enhance doing.

Instead, implementation makes the difference. Every school proved what everyone already knows: doing the same thing gets the same results, and one must therefore swiftly and surely do something different to get better results. Implementation is the one thing that a school seeking to change bar results must do.

We have succeeded already not because we had the best theory, most-committed people, magic insight, best educational partner, most money, or best students but because we implemented. We changed, swiftly and surely, yes wisely, with good data and theory and people to back it up, but change was the point.

Here's a difference, though, to our past and coming success: the success has been and will be because of you--not BarNow, BarBri, Adaptibar, or other for-profit provider, nor educational or state-bar partner, board or alumni initiative, nor leadership or management strategy, but what you do differently in the classroom.

And here's a significant advantage that we have: not only theory, practice, urgency, and new work drive but new tools--a dozen different immediate, substantive, weekly tools for every one of thirteen MBE-tested courses, available now or in template form for any of us to develop, refine, and deploy.

You should in the coming days receive abstracts of the publication's five summaries. But their message is clear: embrace your efficacy. Success is up to you. And the good thing about that? When you win, the reward will be yours, not a for-profit provider, state-bar partner, board, alum, or management group. Go win.
Nelson

Enhancing Classroom Instruction No. 25: FIU's Success
[Research] [09/11/19]
Good morning, MBE-tested-course professors. Please accept this brief article analysis, drawn from Florida International University College of Law's summary, in the National Conference of Bar Examiners' latest quarterly publication, of their bar-exam success.

First, though, consider two qualifiers. One, FIU hasn't had quite the recent dramatic bar-exam improvement about which you may have heard, at least in this sense. Before any bar-exam intervention, FIU admits it was already "about 5% above" the statewide pass-rate average. It was already a succeeding school, not a failing school. FIU was already well ahead, already winning. Its recent success was thus just increasing significantly its above-average rate, not turning around a challenged program. Second, FIU is not an appropriate comparison for us. Its median LSAT was 155 to 156 over the past decade, more like MSU than this law school, which is at least ten points lower in profile than FIU. FIU has never faced the learning challenge that we face every term.

That said, FIU credits its success to something we and many other law schools have also done for many years, which is to train students in metacognition. FIU says it helps students focus on "self-actualized, formative assessment," "self-testing," and "self-regulated learning" to "build better learners by keeping the responsibility with the learner." We, too, have for years coached students in sound study habits, offering many voluntary, formative resources, generally finding that students who use them indeed succeed, while students who don't use them don't succeed-- the problem being usage, not availability. Significantly, FIU dictates no method but instead encourages students to "make autonomous choices about their learning." Yet FIU also acknowledges that "dozens of variables" likely affect bar passage, concluding its summary with the vague exhortation that law professors thus need to dedicate full time to "gaining the expert knowledge necessary to make a real difference in bar passage."

One finds in the article a few more-specific clues in FIU's summary of what they actually do. And here, we can glean some sound encouragement. For one, "from orientation until the last day of classes," they de-emphasize rereading texts as "one of the least effective ways to encode knowledge," producing only "the illusion of mastery...." Instead, somehow, in a manner or by methods that FIU does not here clearly describe, FIU professors "from day one ... focus most heavily upon ... retrieval practice" rather than rereading outlines. What that retrieval practice involves, other than more-frequent testing, much of it apparently self-guided, FIU doesn't clearly say. Yet again, the summary in at least three places stresses de-emphasizing outlines in favor of more-engaged practices of unclear kind, especially employing frequent testing for "the testing effect."

Much of what FIU's summary discloses seems sound, even if by now pretty traditional and in this summary quite non-specific. The key, though, is to get students doing the retrieval practice, not just exhorting them to do it. The classroom is the only place that we have in which we can directly influence what students do. If they must practice, space, and interleave retrieval, then let's find dynamic ways to have all students, especially those who would not or could not follow our advice outside the classroom, do so when they are most under our influence: in the classroom. Applaud FIU's success, but don't think they've found any panacea. They admit that they have not. Their best advice? Stop "[r]elying on lore, intuition, and old assumptions...." Change and implement change, now. I hope you find something helpful here.
Nelson
P.S. Next summary: UMass.

18

Enhancing Classroom Instruction No. 26: UMass's Success
[Research] [09/12/19]
Good morning, MBE-tested-course professors. Please accept this brief analysis of the University of Massachusetts School of Law's summary of their bar-exam success, published in the most-recent quarterly issue of The Bar Examiner, the publication of the National Conference of Bar Examiners.

Unlike FIU, which focuses on science-based enhancements having to do with encoding, retrieval practice, spaced practice, interleaving, and the like, UMass focuses instead on fostering a "community of learning." Students "need to feel supported" if they are to learn, UMass writes. Notably, on LSAT measure, UMass is a closer comparator to this school than FIU is. UMass years ago had a 144 to 145 median LSAT, although that LSAT median rose to 148 in more-recent years, which may explain in part its recent success.

To help students feel supported, UMass does pretty much the opposite of FIU's self-regulated approach, in which FIU says it requires (mandates) nothing of students because to do so disables them. UMass instead requires student to participate in a first-year skills lab and third-year bar-prep course. To UMass, feeling supported in part means forced remediation. The required first-year skills lab "teach[es] and reinforce[s] essential skills and begins to relate those skills to classroom learning...," the article relates without further detail. Beyond the required skills lab and third-year bar-prep course, UMass also offers stipends to graduates to study for the bar rather than work, offers graduates free bar-enrichment programs like this school offers, and negotiates with commercial bar-prep companies for additional graduate services.

Nothing in UMass's summary sounds especially new or unusual. Instead, UMass's work sounds a lot like what this school has for years done, with the required Introduction to Law course and multiple required and voluntary pre-graduation and post-graduation bar-prep courses. UMass's success using those methods should encourage the school to persist with those labs and seminars and extra bar-prep offerings.

But in a time demanding change, another possibility exists. What you seem willing to do differently now is to move from an emphasis on remediation programs outside of doctrinal, substantive-law courses, to enhancing instruction within courses. Enhanced instruction within courses can eliminate the need for remediation outside of courses. The school has already done it here successfully. Indeed, to a degree, those outside seminars, workshops, labs, and other extra sessions may be evidence that courses are not providing the enriched instruction that they can. Moreover, when those outside offerings are voluntary, often the students who need them most won't or can't attend.

So keep on with your effort at enhanced instruction in these MBE-tested courses. You are on to a change in a time when change is not just valuable but necessary. Keep at it.
Nelson
P.S. Tomorrow: UNH's success.

Enhancing Classroom Instruction No. 27: UNH's Success
[Research] [09/13/19]
Good morning, MBE-tested-course professors. Please accept this brief analysis of the University of New Hampshire School of Law's summary of their bar-exam success, published in the most-recent quarterly issue of The Bar Examiner, the publication of the National Conference of Bar Examiners.

Appreciate that UNH is not a particularly good comparator for this law school because of its 154 to 157 LSAT median, more like FIU and MSU than UMass and this law school, a good ten points lower. That said, UNH's approach has been different than FIU, UMass, or this law school. In sum, UNH requires every student to achieve a target score on what it calls a *preliminary bar*. First-year students who do not meet the target score take the preliminary bar again as a second-year student, while some third-year students voluntarily retake the practice bar.

In UNH's case, an outside provider prepares and scores the exam, testing in multiple-choice and essay formats only on contracts, torts, property, and civil procedure, and in performance-test format on any topic but with all relevant law provided. The summary says that the benefit to students lies in the detailed feedback to student and advisor, who together use the results to choose additional coursework, work with remedial instructors on things like time management and IRAC analysis, and alter study techniques, especially better outlining and more practice problems.

UNH's assessment model looks like some of what this law school has done, although this law school ceded its assessment to an outside provider only very recently, and that assessment is voluntary and not comprehensive, whereas UNH ceded its program-enhancement to the for-profit provider some time ago, makes that extra student work mandatory, and treats it as comprehensive. UNH's already-much-higher admissions profile probably makes its assessment model sensible. It knows most of its students are going to do fine and needs only to identify the few who are not, to significantly improve its bar success.

By contrast, this law school has many more students whom the school knows need to make large academic improvements in law school. Here, those students may be the rule or norm rather than the exception. Identifying them without doing a lot more, especially in the classroom, may not be helping much. UNH hasn't found the magic bullet, and the bullet it's using probably isn't the best one for this law school's much-larger bar-improvement target. Let's pursue thoroughgoing enhancement rather than add-on, outside-provider reform.
Nelson
P.S. Next up, UNC.

Enhancing Classroom Instruction No. 28: UNC's Success
[Research] [09/16/19]
Good morning, MBE-tested-course professors. Please accept this brief analysis of the University of North Carolina School of Law's summary of their bar-exam success, published in the most-recent quarterly issue of The Bar Examiner, the publication of the National Conference of Bar Examiners.

I am not sure why The Bar Examiner included UNC because it sports a 161 to 163 LSAT median and so should expect at least the fourteen-points-above-average bar results that its article touts. Nothing special there. What could this law school do with that entering profile? Nevertheless, UNC says that it emphasizes "rigorous and supportive" (is that an oxymoron?) first-year legal writing, expanded third-year bar-prep courses, and two third-year flipped-classroom applied-legal-concepts courses that an outside bar-prep vendor structured for them.

Those flipped-classroom courses share the lectures online before class rather than gathering students to listen to lecture, and then have students work on problems, including bar-style multiple-choice and essay questions, in class. Doing bar-exam questions in class isn't my idea of an engaging classroom. I'd prefer paired exercises that speed the practice and feedback, and that stage and sequence the learning from simple to complex, in a way that bar-exam multiple-choice and essays do not do.

Reading between the lines, I don't think that UNC's faculty made big changes to what they do in the classroom but instead gave others, including their outside bar-prep vendor, greater access to serve students remedially. Unlike FIU, UNC's article mentions nothing of improved learning theory, for instance. And other than increased credit hours for first-year writing, UNC appears to require nothing of its students, not a preliminary bar like UNH nor a skills lab like UMass. That's what a law school can do with a 163 median LSAT. Nothing much to see here, folks. Find inspiration elsewhere.
Nelson
P.S. Last one, Utah, up next.

Enhancing Classroom Instruction No. 29: Utah's Success
[Research] [09/17/19]
Good morning, MBE-tested-course professors. Please accept this brief analysis of the University of Utah College of Law's summary of their bar-exam success, published in the most-recent quarterly issue of The Bar Examiner, the publication of the National Conference of Bar Examiners.

With an LSAT median between 158 and 161 recently, Utah has a student academic profile more like UNC than FIU or UNH, and not much at all like UMass and this law school. Utah says its initiative moved its bar-pass rate from 81% to 90%, the latter figure from a single administration. Considering the relatively wide swings in results even at higher-profile schools, it's hard to rely on that data as proof of success. Yet what did Utah do?

Utah says it increased faculty time for academic support, added a second-year writing class, and offered a third-year bar-prep course for at-risk students. Utah also says that it "encourag[ed] faculty to work more closely and individually" with struggling students, "encouraged all faculty members to expand formative assessments," and "ensured that our curriculum covered key bar exam topics without 'teaching to the test....'"

These actions don't sound like unusual or especially inspired reforms. This law school has long emphasized academic support, faculty support of individual students, and an instructional focus on bar-exam topics. Our doing more of what Utah did wouldn't differentiate us from what we've done. Instead, we might commit again to the kind of engaged in-class practice, forcing frequent, spaced, and interleaved retrieval with prompt feedback, on which FIU has focused and that learning science appears to recommend.

That path is a faculty's can-do proposition, something that we can achieve without relinquishing our responsibility and opportunity to others. We don't need to declare inability, forcing administrators, as in other law schools, to bring on for-profit providers to do work that we could be doing. We are smart and committed enough to succeed at teaching and learning. That's the heartening message to draw from this series of articles. Keep at it.
Nelson

Enhancing Classroom Instruction No. 30: Giving and Taking Feedback
[Research] [09/18/19]
Good morning, MBE-tested-course professors. Attached for your interest is an abstract of a book by two law professors and a communications consultant on the subject of feedback, that President McGrath recommended for our review. We give (or should give) lots of feedback and so should know how best to do so.

While the attached abstract summarizes the 300-page text, here are six quick tips from it that also appear in your shared quick-tips file:

1. help students separate the personal (obstacle) side of feedback from the impersonal (constructive, helpful);
2. distinguish when you are appreciating from when you are coaching and when you are evaluating;
3. be clear with students on the data you reviewed or observation you made when giving feedback;

4. ascribe student behavior to the situation (its stimuli, rewards, consequences), not student character;
5. help students distinguish feedback's constructive message from a harsh messenger triggering bad reaction; and
6. help students acquire a tough, growth-oriented, mistakes-aren't-condemnation attitude.

I hope you find something of value in the attached abstract. Feedback is everywhere. As law professors, we should know something about how to give it and how to take it. Enjoy the rest of the week.
Nelson

Enhancing Classroom Instruction No. 31: Defeating the Knowledge Illusion
[Research] [09/19/19]
Good morning, MBE-tested-course professors. Please accept this encouragement around the article at this link that President McGrath shared last week, on how "smooth-talking professors can lull students into thinking that they've learned more than they have," creating what educators are calling the "knowledge illusion." The article recommends more active engagement in classrooms.

What, though, is an effective way to actively engage students in class? We've probably all had the unfortunate experience of wasting precious class time in case studies, role plays, or other activities that in the end don't seem to provide the consistent level of on-topic engagement for all students with prompt feedback. The challenge is to find the specific activities' best forms.

Each form can have its own value. Single-case studies, an activity that can take a half hour on a single topic or rule, may foster deep reflection and problem solving, which is good, but may not provide comprehensive practice by all students of multiple rules. Flashcards can cover all or nearly all rules, engaging every student with instant feedback, but do not provide deep reflection, application, or problem solving.

My current favorite form is an application exercise that students practice in pairs, requiring that they quickly evaluate within about five minutes up to twenty-five scenarios applying up to four or five different rules, with the answers and applicable rules on the form's back for instant feedback.

This exercise always produces full engagement and concentration with just the right level of interaction. See the attached example on the exclusionary rule, one of several designed for Criminal Procedure on that topic.

To ensure that you are engaging all students, consider varying, sequencing, and staging engagement forms like the attached one. But above all, to defeat the knowledge illusion, engage students around exercises that require them to recall knowledge and demonstrate its application. Show them how much and how little they know, under circumstances where the showing is learning. Enjoy enhancing instruction.
Nelson

Enhancing Classroom Instruction No. 32: Drafting Help
[Resources] [09/20/19]
Good morning, MBE-tested-course professors. Please accept this renewed offer to help you develop and deploy in-class exercises that speed practice and feedback. Responding to the survey last month, several of you asked for help drafting in-class exercises. Attached are these exercises since produced:

1. ninety-five pages of Criminal Procedure exercises including Definitions, Comprehensiveness, Application, and Factors-Practice exercises for all thirteen weeks;

2. one-hundred-seventeen pages of Property II exercises including Definitions, Comprehensiveness, Application, Factors-Practice, and Discrimination exercises for all thirteen weeks;

3. ninety-five pages of Evidence exercises including Definitions, Comprehensiveness, Application, and Factors-Practice exercises for all thirteen weeks;

4. twenty-one pages of Contracts II exercises including Definitions, Issue Spotting, Comprehensiveness, and Problem-Solving exercises for conditions, parol evidence, and third-party rights.

The offer was earnest, urgent, and serious: if you want weekly exercises of any type in any course on any topic or all topics, then please let me know. Our success depends on engaging students in class around studies

that require prompt, accurate recall and correct application, with instant feedback. Thank you for your interest.
Nelson

Enhancing Classroom Instruction No. 33: Considering Incentives
[Methods] [09/23/19]
Good morning, MBE-tested-course professors. This email offers a link to a brief video on how incentives shape what students do outside of class (and in class, too).

You may have realized years ago that exhorting students to study more is not enough. Incentives to work, care for family, care for one's self, or do other things outside of class can simply be more powerful than our advice that more study is necessary.

One way to address competing incentives is to bring critical study activities, like intense performance practice with instant feedback, into class where we have more control (even if not complete control) over incentives.

Fill class time with highest-value studies. If students must forego or choose to forego some, most, or all studies outside of class, then you may still have helped them reach competency or at least get closer. You may also be showing them how to best use their limited study time outside of class. Consider the video, and enjoy the week.
Nelson

Enhancing Classroom Instruction No. 34: In-Class Problems
[Methods] [09/24/19]
Good morning, MBE-tested-course professors. This email offers a link to a brief video on the kind of problems to use for in-class exercises that increase relevant performances with increased feedback.

To engage students in class requires offering some form of problem-based worksheet, exercise, or activity. The temptation is to use multiple-choice questions or essay questions for the in-class problems. Yet these forms are inefficient for in-class exercises.

26

I've several times taught a whole course around in-class and out-of-class multiple-choice questions, where I discovered how slow and difficult they can be to use in class, how little interaction they produce between students, and how hard teaching concepts from them can be.

Better forms use shorter scenarios and require quicker recall and application. Better forms produce a dozen, two dozen, or more performances with instant feedback, every five to ten minutes. You have better forms available to you. Consider the video. And enjoy the week.
Nelson

Enhancing Classroom Instruction No. 35: Shaping Stimuli
[Methods] [09/25/19]
Good morning, MBE-tested-course professors. Please consider watching this brief video on the critical value of frequent shaping stimuli.

We know that students benefit from feedback. We usually think of feedback as associated with assessment, when instead assessment is often a difficult way to supply feedback because of the delay involved between performance and response. What good is feedback a week later, when you and students have already moved on to the next topic?

Thus, think instead of how you can structure activities to provide instant feedback that actually influences, or shapes, student performance. One exam with feedback several days later may do little to improve student performance, whereas instant feedback in well-designed in-class exercises, may provide far greater benefit, correcting and confirming student performance as it occurs.

Shaping stimuli provide instant or near-instant performance feedback, which is the primary form of consistently effective instruction. Watch the brief video for more encouragement on this important subject. And enjoy the rest of the week.
Nelson

Enhancing Classroom Instruction No. 36: Demonstrating Discrimination
[Methods] [09/26/19]

Good morning, MBE-tested-course professors. Please consider watching this brief video on improving student discrimination of legal rules through in-class exercises.

Students often misstate legal rules in ways that over generalize them or under generalize them. By leaving out conditions or misstating definitions, students make the rules apply too broadly or too narrowly. Read your latest set of essay answers, and you will see those errors in recall and precise statement of rules.

We should therefore consider deploying exercises, like the discrimination exercises the sample exercises offer you, that require students to assess rule statements to supply missing terms and conditions, to correct over- and under-generalized rules.

Watch the video for an example of a discrimination exercise that helps students practice precise recall, evaluation, and application of rules, to identify and correct over and under generalization. And enjoy the rest of the week.
Nelson

Enhancing Classroom Instruction No. 37: Sharing Success
[Assessment] [09/27/19]
Good day, MBE-tested-course professors. Please accept these brief endorsements of in-class engagement that two professors from other campuses shared in the past few weeks.

One professor wrote, "I just finished my grades for my past section..., and I wanted to share with you because I think my activities ... ([drawn] from the Western grad assistants) make all the difference. Out of 18 students, I had 9 A or A-, with the lowest grade a B- [excluding one outlier facing outside issues]. ... I was so excited. I attribute this to all the unique activities ... , minimal lecturing, tons of debate and on-your-feet exercises, as well as incorporating multiple-choice practice into every one of my class sessions. ... My class average grade was [above a 3.00]. ... [I]t's exciting when you see the grades go up--it makes me hopeful bar passage will follow...."

Another professor wrote, "I started using [in-class] exercises last term and adapting ... exercises for my ... class last term. []One of the exercises that I added was flashcards. I must admit that I was unsure how students would feel doing 'flashcards' in a law-school class, but they LOVE it, and so do I. They feel a sense of accomplishment, and I know they are learning rules/definitions better. My plan is to continually tweak exercises each term and add interactive exercises each term until I get to an hour per class."

You are as committed, earnest, resourceful, open, and innovative as advertised. Congratulations on embracing the next challenge so speedily and heartily, and keep up the great work.
Nelson

Enhancing Classroom Instruction No. 38: Table of Messages
[Resources] [09/30/19]
Good morning, MBE-tested-course professors. Please accept this message sharing a link to a table of the thirty-seven daily messages so far, in the event that you wish to review any of those messages or locate their resources.

The table shows that collective efforts so far have been to share resources, research, and methods. Your work is creative, singular, challenging, vital, and rewarding. Together, we help one another make that work more so.

Please keep sharing your inspiration, challenges, and successes, and especially your enhancements. Sharing ideas is good, changing because of them is better. Enjoy the week.
Nelson
P.S. The table includes messages coming in the next couple of weeks.

Enhancing Classroom Instruction No. 39: Generation Effect
[Research] [10/01/19]
Good morning, MBE-tested-course professors. Please accept a couple more abstracts (the last two abstracts at pages ten and eleven of the attached file) of meta-analyses of dozens of studies, supporting *two strongly positive learning effects* that we are pursuing through our in-class-engagement enhancements.

29

The first meta-analysis confirms from eighty-six studies the value of the generation effect. *Any activity that you undertake in the classroom that requires student effort has a positive effect on later exam scores* (positive effect on learning), even an activity as mundane as correcting swapped letters in a reading. Of course, generation that involves recalling and applying rules has greater effect. When you help all students employ effort in class to generate responses, such as orally to one another or in brief writings, you help them learn. Effortful presence is routinely better than passive presence.

The second meta-analysis focuses on the value of the in-class test effect: "Research has shown that *implementing frequent low-stakes practice tests in the classroom can lead to a substantial boost in performance on exams* in actual classroom settings." The testing need not be formal exams or quizzes. Any test, even a single question the student answers by writing on a postcard or sharing with a seatmate, or even flashcards, has positive effect over passive presence. Prompt feedback, sharing answers for students to self-correct, is also important. Testing at intervals such as from the prior week enhances the recall effect.

In-class effort is where we have been focusing and need to continue to focus. Base enhancements in controlled studies. The attached abstract is also already available to you as a shared file. The full studies are at pages 71 and 78 of this link. Enjoy the week.
Nelson

Enhancing Classroom Instruction No. 40: More Feedback on Feedback
[Research] [10/02/19]
Good morning, MBE-tested-course professors. Please accept this supplementation of feedback research, drawn from seven law-journal articles that Kim O'Leary shares with us, abstracts of which are attached and in the shared Abstracts file.

These articles, like James' recommended book on feedback abstracted for you last month, show the power that our feedback has not only on student success but also on their mental and emotional health into practice. In addition to the attached abstracts, I have also updated the shared Quick Tips file with these tips:

1. help students develop their receiving-feedback, incorporating-feedback skill;
2. show students that employers desire that their new hires receive feedback well;
3. discourage negative, excuse-making reactions to feedback;
4. encourage solicitation of feedback;
5. disarm feedback resistance by beginning with praise of positive performance;
6. disarm feedback resistance by requesting self-critique;
7. disarm feedback resistance by reinforcing and amplifying self-critique;
8. give more feedback than merely supplying a model answer;
9. supply rubrics and individual feedback along with annotated model answers;
10. establish and publish clear performance criteria and standards;
11. your individualized feedback can improve performance in other courses;
12. offer varied, autonomy-supportive instruction with constructive feedback.

I hope that you find something helpful here. Enjoy the day, while knowing that your feedback words, tone, and style with students have powerful impact.
Nelson

Enhancing Classroom Instruction No. 41: Calculating Discrimination
[Assessment] [10/03/19]
Good day, MBE-tested-course professors. Please consider the following method that Kim O'Leary calls to our attention for calculating the discrimination value for your multiple-choice questions.

As a reminder, discrimination measures how effectively the question separates strong performers from weak performers. To be valid and reliable, and helpful in measuring how effectively students are studying, questions should generally have top-scoring students getting them right, while some bottom-scoring students get them wrong.

Thus, a question with a perfect +1.00 discrimination would have all top-scoring students getting the question correct while all bottom-scoring students get the question incorrect. A question with a perfectly perverse -

31

1.00 discrimination value would have all top-scoring students getting the question wrong while all bottom-scoring students get the question correct. Depending on the instruction's goal, well-designed questions generally have at least a +.25 discrimination value.

To calculate the discrimination value on your multiple-choice questions, create a spreadsheet with students listed down the left side (in rows) and questions across the top (in columns). Then, going through each exam, put a 1 in each box for each question that each student gets correct, and a 0 for each incorrect question. It won't take long if you persevere... even less time if you ask an administrative assistant to do it for you.

Then, take roughly 25% of the top-ranked scorers on the overall exam, which you can do by including the total correct for each student in an extra column and then sorting the full table on that column. So if you have forty students, you'd be taking the top ten students. Also take the same number (ten in this example) of bottom-ranked students.

Then, for each question, count the 1s for the top 25% of students and the 1s for the bottom 25% of students. Subtract the bottom-25% total from the top-25% total. Then divide that number by the number of students in the top group (or bottom group, those numbers being the same). The fraction your calculation produces, between -1 and +1, is that question's discrimination score.

Use the scores to eliminate or fix questions with negative discrimination because they are misleading strong students. Make questions with zero discrimination value harder if you believe that the bar exam is indeed harder. Make questions with high-positive discrimination scores above .40 or .50 easier or clearer if you believe the bar exam is easier or clearer. Consider equating all items to the difficulty of the bar exam.
Nelson

Enhancing Classroom Instruction No. 42: Flashcard Use
[Assessment] [10/04/19]
Good morning, MBE-tested-course professors. Please take sixty seconds (less for most of you) to answer this survey on whether and how you recommend flashcard use.

Flashcards, when designed and used properly, can produce significant gains in fluent (fast and accurate) concept recall. Students know so, although when left on their own, they may purchase poorly designed flashcards or make their own of unhelpful design and use them poorly.

The memory advantage of flashcards over outlines has to do with eliminating the surrounding prompts that outlines supply. Of course, a student can remember what comes next on an outline after staring at it for hours. The problem is that exams don't supply the surrounding prompts.

Well-designed flashcards can isolate and randomize the knowledge, forcing students to use mental effort (the generation effect!) to recall any concept swiftly and accurately without other surrounding concepts first prompting it. Let's see how many of us see value in this study-recommended practice. Enjoy.
Nelson

Enhancing Classroom Instruction No. 43: In-Class Exercises
[Assessment] [10/07/19]
Good morning, MBE-tested-course professors. Please take 90 seconds (less for most of you) to answer this brief survey on whether you use in-class exercises and if so then how often and in what form, so that we can share our progress in anonymous fashion.

Our initiative is to increase engagement in class because of the competing outside-of-class incentives (work, family, health, and yes other distraction including play) that keep many students from doing all that they should.

Moving from passive to active classroom then the constructive classroom and finally the interactive classroom increases learning. Students don't necessarily feel as if they learn more because of the striving that engagement takes, but they are learning more, the effort being exactly the point.

Have you taken the plunge? And if so, then how often and how? Let's find out how we are doing collectively. Thank you, and enjoy the week.
Nelson

Enhancing Classroom Instruction No. 44: Assessment of Assessment
[Assessment] 10/08/19]
Good morning, MBE-tested-course colleagues. Please take three minutes to answer this brief survey, which if you do answer should generate anonymous information to give you a clearer idea how we assessing and why.

Studies show the value of assessment, including taking advantage of the test effect while defeating the procrastination curve. Assessment with prompt feedback is even better because it guides and corrects learning.

But assessment poses obstacles, too, some real, some likely solvable or reducible, while others we may be imagining. Where are you currently on assessment, and why? Let's see what we can learn together about our common practices. Enjoy.
Nelson

Enhancing Classroom Instruction No. 45: Professor Approach
[Research] [10/09/19]
Good morning, MBE-tested-course professors. Please consider a brief note about attitude--instructor attitude, professor attitude, our attitude. What you think about your subject and students means more than you may think. Study after study shows the positive influence of teacher attitudes on student learning and behavior.

The question isn't just what you know of your subject but also what you convey to students that you think of your subject--and think of them. Conveying to students the broader positive role and purpose of your subject can be the first step to helping students learn it.

Not only must we care about our subjects, but we must also care about students, indeed showing them that we care, not just saying that we care. Showing care includes not just empathy, sensitivity, and compassion, but, more so, organization, prioritization, and teaching effectiveness.

On one measure, the teacher who cares most about students, most-fully demonstrating to students that care, is the teacher who at course end is able to score students the highest, proving that the teacher helped them learn. Students are here to learn, and caring about them is to help them learn.

Students may not even know why they learn or fail to learn, but we can and should know. Moreover, we can and should adapt instruction until students do learn, whether they know why they learn or do not know. Our measure isn't what we know or discuss but how students respond to what we do. Right? Enjoy the week.
Nelson

Enhancing Classroom Instruction No. 46: Improving Resources
[Resources] [10/10/19]
Good morning, MBE-tested-course professors. Please consider this brief message on altering, adapting, and improving shared resources, generated, edited, and proofed by others but shared with you.

Each of you has your own way of recalling, reciting, and phrasing law. Some of you see certain rule exceptions or alternatives as important, while others of you see other rules as more important. One of you corrects something away from what another discerns as already correct.

These variations are healthy, natural, indeed just how law lives, breathes, and adapts. These variations are also unimportant so far as our overall success with students is concerned. We must teach them accurate law, but students have so vastly much to learn that disputes over precisely what they learn in any one specific instance pale to insignificance.

Please feel free to modify any shared resource in any way that better suits your instructional needs. Just don't ignore resources and methods that fully engage students with prompt corrective feedback. Keep exploring, sharing, and adapting. That's what an effective team does. And enjoy the week.
Nelson

Enhancing Classroom Instruction No. 47: Managing Cognitive Load
[Research] [10/11/19]
Good morning, MBE-tested-course professors. Please consider the implications of an important study appearing at page 31 of the book

Applying the Science of Learning, on a subject that should influence law school instruction.

In brief, the study shows how overloading short-term memory reverses (frustrates and defeats) acquisition and demonstration of expertise, in low-knowledge-level learners. To increase learning and build expertise, the instructor must initially limit the student's cognitive load to free working memory to manipulate the concepts.

This science of learning is why the sample application exercises shared with you (example attached) limit fact patterns to a single line, when presenting new topics for students to learn. Limiting cognitive load lets students recall, apply, test, and evaluate the new rules until they have them properly and firmly in place.

When teaching new topics, we need to limit the quantity of information that we require students to hold in working memory while they apply the new concept, so that they can explore how the concept works. When instead we give students complex fact patterns through which to practice application of new knowledge, we limit their ability to learn the new knowledge.

Students can, should, and indeed must learn to decipher complex fact patterns to apply legal rules. Yet they should not have to do so at the same time that they are learning those rules. Consider the value of the attached sample application exercises to introduce the application of new concepts. And enjoy the weekend.
Nelson

Enhancing Classroom Instruction No. 48: Science on Feedback
[Research] [10/14/19]
Good morning, MBE-tested-course professors. Please consider the implications of a helpful summary of studies on the value of feedback, appearing at page 42 of the book *Applying the Science of Learning.*

The psychologist authors point to studies showing that teachers generally believe that they give lots of feedback in class, whereas skilled observers and students find that teachers generally do not. Self-evaluate realistically. Are we giving substantial, consistent, useful, and timely feedback?

36

Meta-analyses show that feedback in class can double the learning (can have twice the effect of any other classroom variable). The reason is not just in the feedback itself. Students simply work harder when they know that they are about to receive timely and helpful feedback. Feedback helps because it measures against stated goals, directing students toward those goals. Feedback also helps because it measures progress toward goals, while suggesting next steps to achieve further progress.

Feedback for novice learners should focus on knowledge *acquisition*. Initially, at the knowledge-acquisition stage, feedback should be within seconds of performance. Feedback for intermediate learners should focus on knowledge *application*. Mastery-level learners should receive feedback on the level of their engagement and quality of work produced.

Feedback should be corrective (negative, failure-identifying) but within the context of positive teacher-student relationships and with the student's understanding that learning requires traveling a distance from initial performance. Don't hesitate to allow for errors, when feedback can correct them. Indeed, design for errors but with prompt correction. Let learners experience failure and correction. I hope you find something useful in this summary of feedback studies. Enjoy the week.
Nelson
P.S. I hope you are occasionally following the link to read or review these full psychology-of-learning articles. They are fascinating.

Enhancing Classroom Instruction No. 49: Application Exercises
[Resources] [10/15/19]
Good morning, MBE-tested-course professors. Please accept this message offering to supply application exercises for all MBE-tested topics in any MBE-tested course, like the attached twenty Contracts II exercises with two-hundred-and-five items or the attached Constitutional Law I exercises with two-hundred-ninety-six items.

These application exercises give students prompt repetitive practice of each concept, with instant feedback. The brevity of the fact patterns help students isolate the concept's critical attributes from its variable attributes without overloading working memory, thus managing cognitive load.

37

While the attached exercises address all topics from the MBE's list, you and I can create and deploy additional application exercises for any distinction in any concept that you wish to teach. You can also ask students in pairs to do these exercises together in class in five minutes, giving them instant engaged practice with very little interruption in your other in-class designs. Hope you find something helpful here. Enjoy the week.

Nelson

Enhancing Classroom Instruction No. 50: Table of Exercises
[Resources] [10/16/19]

Good morning, MBE-tested-course professors. Please accept this link to a shared table of the exercises available to you, in any of the school's thirteen MBE-tested courses.

Exercises are available for every week of Property I, Property II, Torts I, Torts II, Evidence, and Criminal Procedure, and some topics of Contracts II and Criminal Law, while sample exercises are available for all remaining thirteen courses.

I would gladly work with any of you to draft more exercises for any topic in any of these thirteen courses, re-order exercises to your syllabus, and produce full workbooks of these exercises along with flashcards, outlines, and multiple-choice questions.

Let's keep finding ways together to speed the in-class learning of students on these core bar-tested subjects and their many topics, drawing on the generation effect and test-enhanced learning. Enjoy the week.

Nelson

P.S. I will soon have some feedback for you on how many of us acknowledge using exercises in class. If you haven't completed the In-Class Exercises survey, then I hope you will so that my feedback is more accurate and encouraging.

Enhancing Classroom Instruction No. 51: Self-Explanation in the Classroom
[Research] [10/17/19]

Good morning, MBE-tested-course professors. Please accept the attached two abstracts of meta-analyses of classroom studies (at pages eleven and

38

twelve of the attachment), the full articles of which are at pages 91 and 118 in this psychology text. These two articles show how rich in learning the classroom can be.

The first article surveys research on classroom self-explanation, finding that students who more-often explain new knowledge and skills to themselves, and do so with higher-quality insights, learn faster than students who do not self-explain. The authors advocate that instructors move forward along the passive-active-constructive-interactive spectrum, each next level being better than the prior level at enhancing learning because of the greater opportunity for self-explanation.

The second article surveys research on worked examples. Worked examples, like those you used to see in mathematics books, show students how to solve problems before requiring students to do so. Worked examples reduce initial cognitive load so that students can learn the principles, strategies, and imagining that problem solving requires, turning them into heuristics that students can then use for their own problem solving. Once again, moving from a passive classroom to active, constructive, and interactive increases opportunities for worked examples.

I hope you find something from these research abstracts, also available to you in the shared abstracts file. This science may be confirming your own unexpressed sense of how you learn. Whether it does so or not, it proves the value of these methods. Enjoy the rest of the week and weekend.
Nelson

Enhancing Classroom Instruction No. 52: Monitoring In-Class Exercises
[Methods] [10/18/19]
Good morning, MBE-tested-course professors. Please accept this video link showing how students interact during in-class exercises and how you can monitor and evaluate that interaction.

Studies urge that instructors move instruction forward along the passive-active-constructive-interactive spectrum to increase student engagement and learning. The forty-second video at this link shows students doing in-class exercises together in highly interactive fashion.

Notice how students are together doing all of these activities: speaking, listening actively, writing on their own, writing what their seatmate says, nodding in agreement, seconding and supplementing what the other says, looking up information, pointing out information to the other, and checking their surmises against model answers.

Try sustaining this focused interaction recalling and applying the topics just lectured, presented, and discussed, for ten, twenty, forty, or even fifty minutes, using brief interruptions to report out, move to another exercise, change seatmates, and raise points or corrections.

Record students as in this video, for inspiration, monitoring, study, and accountability. And please share with me what you see and discern. Lecturing is fun and easy, while constructing and sustaining these interactive environments is hard, but study after study shows the value of doing the hard over the easy. Enjoy the week.
Nelson

Enhancing Classroom Instruction No. 53: Accomplishing Change
[Research] [10/21/19]
Good morning, MBE-tested-course professors. Please consider this brief note about *accomplishing organizational change*, drawn from a 1996 Harvard Business School publication by its leadership professor John Kotter.

Kotter writes the obvious: organizations fail to change for lack of urgency, failure to create a guiding coalition, underestimating vision's power and then way under-communicating the vision, letting obstacles block the vision, failing to seize and celebrate short-term wins, declaring victory too soon, and failing to anchor changes deep in the organization's culture. Anything sound familiar here?

Committees, subcommittees, task forces, departments, groups, councils, and units do not accomplish change, although they may identify and support change. Workers effect change. You effect change. Nothing changes until enough of us do things differently out of a sense of an urgent need to do so, ensure the changes are effective, stick to those changes long enough to embed them in our practice, and then celebrate them together.

40

I'd like to know more about how we have changed in the classroom in the past ten years, five years, one year, and one term, indeed in the past month or week. Where is our effective coalition--not in a unit or committee or department but in the classroom? What are enough of us doing differently from what we did previously, with demonstrable positive effects? Keep thinking of around what we are coalescing in urgent need.
Nelson

Enhancing Classroom Instruction No. 54: Reminder on Spacing and Interleaving
[Research] [1022/19]
Good morning, MBE-tested-course professors. Please accept this abstract of a chapter at page 131 of this psychology text, reminding us of the value of spacing and interleaving student studies.

The psychologist author summarizes the abundant research on the value of spacing rather than massing studies and interleaving (mixing) rather than blocking studies. Spreading study and recall out over time, rather than concentrating studies into a single window, increases the accuracy and quantity of recall. Mixing one aspect of a subject with another aspect, moving back and forth between aspects rather than studying each aspect only in a single block, increases the accuracy and quantity of recall. The author gives several study examples of the high value of each strategy.

The author then lists ways to draw on these strategies. First, mix bits of review into your lecture or discussion of new topics. Drop a problem or two from a prior week into each set of problems on new topics. Test students frequently over topics learned in the prior three weeks and, toward the course's end, three months, requiring them to revisit topics learned but promptly set aside and forgotten. Randomize problems across multiple recent topics rather than block them into single topics.

Students will perceive that these and other spacing and interleaving practices slow them down and require more effort, as they struggle to recall and as they refer to note or other prior resources. That's precisely the strategies' value. Students will feel that they are learning less, but explain that they are learning more, their increased effort being the

41

reliable indication. Spacing and interleaving present challenges to both instructors designing curriculum and to students when studying, which is why instruction tends to avoid it even though studies prove it effective. Don't let the challenges discourage you or students. Space and interleave. Space and interleave. And enjoy the week.
Nelson

Enhancing Classroom Instruction No. 55: Quick Tips
[Research] [10/23/19]
Good morning, MBE-tested-course professors. Please consider making a quick review of the growing Quick Tips file at this link, now offering about sixty one-line tips for enhancing instruction, each tip drawn from one of the research books, chapters, or articles in the abstracts file.

Enhancing instruction is not a matter of finding a single magic bullet. You have repeatedly experienced the phenomenon of how widely varying strategies, activities, and resources help different students differently.

I once surveyed students on their view of the value of twenty different resources and activities, expecting to find that most students favored a couple or few prominent things that I preferred and viewed as the most valuable. Instead, students distributed their interests across all things.

We could, in other words, adopt all of the quick tips, or at least a wide variety of them, to enhance instruction and serve students well. Keep exploring, keep adding, keep experimenting, and keep adopting while cautiously culling and discarding. Let your instruction evolve into a rich and complex organism. Doesn't it seem that way? Enjoy the week.
Nelson

Enhancing Classroom Instruction No. 56: Student Self-Perceptions
[Research] [10/24/19]
Good morning, MBE-tested-course professors. Please accept this abstract of a chapter at page 142 of this psychology text, urging instructors to help students better self-evaluate because of their generally poor, overly optimistic self-perceptions. This abstract and all other offered abstracts are also available at this link.

The psychologist authors review research showing that students often err in evaluating their own learning, with the result that they learn more poorly. Errors in self-evaluation of learning lead to poor student choices in study practices. Students believe that they know more than they know, their self-evaluations often too positive. Overconfidence exists not just among top students but also among failing students. Students may strive in studies but not strive to evaluate their studies. They let things fall where they may, failing to adjust study practices based on their actual state of skill and knowledge.

Students should instead work equally hard at meta-cognitive monitoring. Instructors should offer frequent opportunities for student self-evaluation, while directing students toward high-value strategies like spacing and interleaving studies, self-quizzing, and self-explanation. Help students choose measurable mastery goals, like reaching certain scores on certain objective practice exams. Foster a culture and design the tools for students to fail, study, and succeed. Encourage risk-taking studies in which students learn the accurate measure of their knowledge and skill. Encourage students to see learning as incremental, fail-study-succeed, rather than attribute based, like some are smart and others are not.

Are you offering, indeed requiring, frequent self-evaluation against objective measures. Do students in your course know where they stand before they take graded exams? Are they adjusting studies toward higher-value activities? Help students see themselves as they are rather than as they want to be. Then, they'll become whom they want to be. Nelson

Enhancing Classroom Instruction No. 57: From Purpose to Excellence
[Morale] [10/25/19]
Good morning, MBE-tested-course professors. Please accept these brief thoughts, drawn from a lost source, on the process of continuous improvement.

We improve our resources and methods because we have a clear and valued purpose, which is that students learn law efficiently and effectively to qualify for profitable and socially productive law practice.

That purpose germinates in us a certain curiosity, an urge or restlessness that we discover ever-better means for achieving our purpose. We wake and rest with a passion, unease, or ardent spirit to do otherwise, to do more, to do differently, in pursuit of our purpose.

As we sate that curiosity through research and experimentation, we grow in excellence, achieving more with students than we previously thought possible. And that growth in excellence further fuels our purpose because we see its achievement as possible. We embrace our own efficacy.

Keep pursuing this circle from purpose through curiosity to excellence and back to purpose. Don't lose sight of who you are and what you are accomplishing. And enjoy the weekend.
Nelson

Enhancing Classroom Instruction No. 58: Meta-Cognitive Practices
[Research] [10/28/19]
Good morning, MBE-tested-course professors. Please accept this brief abstract of a research review at page 152 of this psychology text, urging that instructors help students develop and draw on their meta-cognitive capacity.

Psychology defines meta-cognition as *self-monitoring and regulation of cognitive processes in pursuit of a goal.* While one cannot observe meta-cognition, and its operation is thus ambiguous, studies show that meta-cognitive practices can enhance learning. Yet students differ in their meta-cognitive development, begun at an early age and continued through adulthood. Helping students draw on and develop their meta-cognitive practices is thus important to instruction.

Meta-cognition involves both knowledge about one's self and one's thinking, that is, the ability to state true things about thinking, and then the ability or willingness to regulate one's development through activities like planning and assessment. Knowledge without regulation, or regulation based on incorrect knowledge, doesn't work. One critical form of meta-cognition is prediction of knowing, that is, the student's accuracy as to the state of their current knowledge and skill relative to exam standards. Better-performing students have better predictive meta-cognition. They are more accurate in saying how they will perform on a

44

test. The greater the student's sophistication in beliefs about learning, the greater the meta-cognitive capacity.

One approach to improving meta-cognition is to have students explicitly question themselves and others with whom they study, asking what they are doing, why they are doing it, and how it is helping them. They may, for instance, be discerning the problem, exploring solution methods, planning the solution process, implementing the solution process, or verifying their solution's accuracy. Another suggestion is to encourage students to consider their meta-cognitive practices, teach them those practices, and through instructional design help them maintain those practices.

Specific techniques can include having students first assess their knowledge level, then identify the most-difficult concept, keep a self-reflective journal on meta-cognition, and integrate self-reflection into scored assignments with questions like what was the most challenging concept and most-effective approach to mastering it. Grouping students to learn meta-cognitive practices from and with one another can also help. Don't hesitate to instruct in meta-cognition. Indeed, design and enhance to push students to self-evaluate and regulate their learning. And enjoy the week.
Nelson

Enhancing Classroom Instruction No. 59: Coalescing Around Engagement
[Assessment] [10/29/19]
Good morning, MBE-tested-course professors. Please accept this report of results of two surveys of the thirty-eight of us. The findings suggest some coalescing around in-class engagement forms.

Twelve of the thirty-eight of us, or about one third, participated in the surveys. Eleven of the twelve survey participants reported using in-class exercises, eight using those exercises weekly, two most weeks, and one some weeks. If around one-third of us (nearly all responding to the survey) are engaging students regularly or often in class, then that number and percentage represents a substantial overall influence. I am aware that three other professors not responding to the survey also use in-class exercises, making for fourteen of thirty-eight, or somewhat more than a third.

45

The survey shows that the forms of exercise vary widely, which is wonderful, although (and this finding is the best) all professors using in-class exercises have all students participating at once, and all provide instant feedback. One third of you are finding ways to get all students practicing in class with feedback. The variety of exercises goes well beyond the eight offered forms, although several use offered forms, and nine offer flashcards (half for in-class use). You are both trusting of offered resources and creative in deploying other forms.

In-class engagement of all students is a huge gain. For a decade and a half, I have observed many of the law school's best lecturers, best Socratic examiners. I have also sat with teaching-and-learning experts, watching them evaluate some of those lecturers minute by minute, using rigorous means. They conclude, as others conclude, that lectures, while helpful and important, do not engage all students in the constructive manner and to the performance degree, that exercise forms do. Congratulations on your collective engagement of students in their classroom experience. This evidence of your innovation and exploration seems strong. Let's celebrate.
Nelson

Enhancing Classroom Instruction No. 60: Influencing Student Behavior
[Research] [10/30/19]
Good morning, MBE-tested-course professors. Please accept this brief abstract (longer abstract in the shared file) of a psychology text *Influence: Science and Practice* recommended by the WMU grad-student team, to help us influence students into better choices.

Teachers tend to exhort students: *do this because I say it's good for you.* Yet the author's point is that with technology inundating us with information and choices, we are more distracted and less reasoning than ever in our personal choices, especially our allocation of scarce time, and thus more susceptible to the unthinking heuristics by which we make most decisions. Here are a few of the author's phenomenon, along with my suggestions how we might use the phenomenon to help students make better study choices:

1. because we tend to proceed by social proof, doing based on what we see others do rather than as we should do, use student leaders or teaching assistants to adopt and endorse sound studies so that others follow;

2. because we tend to agree to perform when we owe the requester reciprocity, returning favors even when the return is out of proportion to the requester's prior action, do something for students first, even if to make a simple concession, so that they will then do for you as you recommend;

3. because we tend to follow through on commitments that we first make, rather than just doing the right thing, get students to commit to a goal in shared writing, so that they then perform toward the goal, the small act of commitment leading to greater follow through;

4. because we tend to agree with people whom we like more than with people whom we don't like, be more likable to students, or if you cannot, then retain a likable teaching assistant to recommend your preferred study practices, with whom students may then agree;

5. because we tend to do as authority requires us to do, and as experts recommend that we do, show yourself an authority on study techniques, citing the science and research, showing your knowledge of the phenomenon, so that students accept your study recommendations as authoritative;

6. because we tend to value things that are scarce more than things that are abundant, invite sign-ups for limited space or resources, and you'll get more sign-ups, but then be sure that all students get the space or resources and especially that students who need the extra help have access to it.

One can easily see these strategies as manipulative, but one can also see them as arranging the stimuli to influence students into the best choices rather than arranging the stimuli to produce ignorance. Armed with the science, we have the choice. Above all, recognize that our recommendations compete with powerful contrary influences. I hope you find something helpful here. Enjoy the week.
Nelson

Enhancing Classroom Instruction No. 61: Conversation Series
[Methods] [10/31/19]
Good morning, MBE-tested-course professors. Please accept this brief invitation to share a teaching conversation with the rest of us, about how you have been adapting classroom activities to meet the learning challenges that we face every term.

I would like to record your thoughts in a conversation of whatever length you wish, and if we agree afterward, to share it with the rest of us, for listening at convenience. Let's build an oral history reflecting how our commitments shape our classroom development.

The value of doing so is not just for your colleagues to learn from your experience. The value is also to you, listening to yourself articulate insights, learning from your own expression, and maybe learning from echoes others then share with you.

Please just send me a reply email if you are interested, with your best days and times of the weekday, evening, or weekend. Your location doesn't matter. Audio only, from distance. Thank you, and enjoy the week.
Nelson
P.S. Expect in the next couple of days to start hearing some good conversations already recorded.

Enhancing Classroom Instruction No. 62: Conversation with Kim O'Leary
[Methods] [11/01/19]
Good morning, MBE-tested-course professors. Please consider listening at this link to a fifty-minute podcast-style conversation with Kim O'Leary about her recent insights into classroom teaching and learning.

Many of us have learned from Kim over the years, drawing on her clinical-education skills for which she has earned a well-deserved national reputation. Kim's move two years ago into the first-year classroom, now teaching Contracts I and Property II, has given her great opportunity to apply her considerable skill in that classroom testing.

As you might imagine from her clinical background, Kim creates an active, engaged classroom environment. She began her podcast

48

conversation with the foundation that instructors should plan for students to *do*, to perform and practice, so that students learn while both student and instructor can see and monitor progress.

Kim's insights extend well beyond theoretical foundations, though. Her talk includes detail about particulars like paired work, group work and group size, types of activities, and forms of feedback. Most of all, though, one sees Kim's continual exploration, as she put it, in a willingness to try, fail sometimes, but then promptly try again, enhancing instruction.

Appreciate and celebrate Kim and her long commitment to teaching and learning. Draw from her, and share with her. And enjoy the weekend. Nelson

Enhancing Classroom Instruction No. 63: Projecting Student Work
[Methods] [11/04/19]
Good morning, MBE-tested-course professors. Please accept this brief description of how you can, with the school's available technology, project any student work as students proceed with in-class exercises.

Projecting student work adds another level of accountability, excitement, and concentration to in-class exercises, when you can at any moment call out any student pair to share their work on the screen with the whole class for examination and discussion.

All that you need do is to send all students a WebEx invite for the in-class exercise time. Students should accept the invite with their laptop computers, mute audio and video, and go to work together on whatever exercise or problem you present to them.

Project your own WebEx screen using the classroom projection. Then walk around the class, looking at student screen work. When you see something that you want other students to see, especially laudable work, sound solutions, and strong writing and analysis, then ask that student pair to share their screen.

You may have seen special classrooms that have multiple projectors and screens spread around the classroom for all students to project work. You don't need multiple projectors and screens but can instead use WebEx to

project any student work. Imagine the possibilities. Thank you, and enjoy the weekend.
Nelson

Enhancing Classroom Instruction No. 64: Conversation with Brendan Beery
[Methods] [11/05/19]
Good morning, MBE-tested-course professors. Please take due advantage listening to this conversation with our colleague Brendan Beery about classroom engagement.

If you don't know, and you well might not because of the encouraging humility with which he conducts himself, then appreciate that Brendan is among our leaders in thoughtful design of in-class exercises that fully engage students to increase their learning. I invited Brendan to share his work because I saw so many sound things that he was doing. My revelation in engaging Brendan was how intentional, open, and yet discerning he has been in selecting, testing, and shaping those designs. His work frankly humbles me. Picture a classroom in which students immediately engage one another in stimulating retrieval competition, drawing on the principle of spaced repetition, and then engage successively in quick-application and other exercises that a teaching assistant scores in real time for feedback within the same class.

Most impressively, Brendan's students not only enthusiastically embrace their in-class engagement but also request more and extended such designs. They also use the exercises to study and prepare for exams, on which their scores have improved due to the designs. Brendan shows how incredibly complex learning law is and how subtle and multi-dimensioned instruction should be to help students best master that complexity. Truly, I learned things from Brendan's conversation that I am very glad to know, even as he admits that his recent innovations are reinvigorating him in this hard work of helping students learn law. His insights hearten me and will inform and hearten you, too. Please find the time to listen. Thank you, and enjoy the rest of the week.
Nelson

Enhancing Classroom Instruction No. 65: Feedback on Exams Survey.
[Assessment] [11/06/19]
Good morning, MBE-tested-course professors. Please accept this feedback on responses to the survey sent to you last month on your exam practices. Fourteen of the thirty-seven of you responded to the survey, giving us some interesting data to consider.

Most of you (57%) give only two exams, a mid-term and final. So most of us are fairly traditional in exam frequency and distribution. About a quarter (28%) of us, though, give four exams, and a couple more (14%) give five exams. Some of you are making concerted efforts through exams (exams are not the only way) to defeat the procrastination curve, take advantage of the testing effect, space studies (requiring review through the term), and interleave studies (mixing old and new topics).

Interestingly, none of you adopt WMU instructional-design research-lab director Dr. Johnson's recommendation of five equally weighted, twenty-percent-of-the-grade exams. The closest weights the final exam fifty percent, the rest of you giving the final a higher percentage right up to several of you at eighty or ninety percent--traditional for law school. Some reason that weighting the final habituates students to the all-in-one bar exam. Does it prepare them for the bar, though?

Most of you are giving exams with the weight and frequency that you think best, although a couple expressed interest in more research. All of you get exams back within one week, while a few of you commit to getting exams back the same day or next day. Kudos to all such efforts. Most have all you need for administering exams as you think best, although a few would like more time for drafting, more and better help scoring, more class time for assessment, and more or better multiple-choice questions.

Clearly, we all take the assessment challenge seriously. And variety in approaches is good. On the whole, though, we may not be much different from traditional programs, although we do reflect a reasonably wide variety of approaches. Thanks for sharing.
Nelson

Enhancing Classroom Instruction No. 66: Listening to Students.
[Assessment] [11/07/19]
Good morning, MBE-tested-course professors. Please accept this brief note about listening to students, with some survey results.

Students don't always know what's best for them. They may minimize effort, taking the easy route through studies, when effortless learning isn't maximal learning. Engaging, striving, and learning at maximum level can feel fatiguing, even confusing, when instead it produces the greater results. Push students so that they do not fall prey to the knowledge illusion.

Yet students can give us helpful feedback about our methods and resources. I frequently ask students what they feel is working or not working for them, as I suspect you also do. I may not change instruction because of their answers, unless I find validity and reliability in what they say.

Google Forms is a simple way to collect survey information from students. It takes no training to prepare a Form, accessed from your Google Apps grid in Gmail. The Form summarizes responses both individually and in aggregate. Below are responses that I just collected from first-term students answering the question "How, in your own words, do the in-class exercises serve you in learning and applying law concepts?" Enjoy the week.
Nelson

"It's nice to interact with the new material in different ways to identify any gaps in what I've learned while I'm still in class."

"They help give me a better understanding of the material. We typically do the exercises after the hour/before the break so by doing some of the exercises is makes me go back over the material we just learned and makes me apply it to different scenarios, like issue spotting. So, I think it gives me a better understanding and I retain the material better."

"It allows me to constantly see and rewrite the various definitions of the key terms which makes it easier to recall when needed. It also exposes us to a variety of different fact patterns that allows us to think about real life scenarios and how we can apply what we learned so far to each situation. I also like being exposed to simulated paperwork from a real job because it introduces us to the basic day to day operations. This will be helpful later on when starting a new job and having the expectation from those around us of being highly educated in our field."

"The in-class exercises help me practice and remember elements of the law and see how it applies to different hypothetical situations so that I may recognize it more easily in real life. This allows me to understand the bigger picture and retain information easier when I'm working with different rules hands-on, rather than simply reading cases."

Enhancing Classroom Instruction No. 67: Conversation with Victoria Vuletich
[Assessment] [11/08/19]
Good morning, MBE-tested-course professors. Please consider listening to a classroom-engagement conversation, at this link, with our colleague Victoria Vuletich.

This approximately forty-minute conversation immediately makes clear that Victoria has given great eye, ear, and effort to enhancing instruction with classroom exercises and activities that engage students, effectively increasing their learning. The sensitive spirit Victoria carries into her insightful work shines through in her articulation of its grounds and premises.

Victoria uses every student exam to evaluate her instruction. In this conversation, she shares some of what she is doing and, more so, who has helped her (especially Dr. Johnson, his grad-student team, and colleagues) and why she has so pursued her craft so richly. Victoria has immense respect for her colleagues, yes, but the greatest respect for the commitment and value of students.

Lend your own ear to learning's oracle, in this conversation, Dr. Johnson and his grad-student team, the empirical research, and the spirit within you. Take heart in rich craft.
Nelson

Enhancing Classroom Instruction No. 68: Affirming Exercise Variety
[Assessment] [11/11/19]

Good morning, MBE-tested-course professors. Please accept this student response to an in-class survey, in which the student describes the value of offering variety in in-class exercises:

"I have found the in-class exercises, and really, the workbook as a whole, to be a very interesting and useful tool. The benefit of the exercises, in my opinion, is that *it allows you to approach the same body of knowledge from different perspectives. Some exercises may give greater clarity on a subject, some will draw out the nuanced differences between theories, and others will simply drive home the basic elements. The more difficult exercises, such as problem-solving ones, really challenge you to think creatively with the material. Different people think differently, so not all exercises will be as useful to everyone, but that's why its great to have so many options.* I struggle with the discrimination exercise for some reason, but I can tell from the other exercises that I know the material, so I don't worry about using that exercise. Other people, like my seat partner, does really well that that exercise, so it's good to have the variety. The use of class time for the exercises is beneficial in that it forces us to talk the material out with another student, which we wouldn't typically have the opportunity to do easily especially as night students. Also, it's good to have the professor and TA there to ask some of the clarifying questions that the exercises should and do generate."

Students, even ones like this one who works full-time, will take time to give you valuable feedback on instruction. Ask, listen, and adapt. And when something's working, hone it, improve it. Let students help you confirm and correct, while sticking to the science. Enjoy the weekend. Nelson

Enhancing Classroom Instruction No. 69: Evidence of Learning
[Assessment] [11/12/19]
Good morning, MBE-tested-course professors. Please accept this invitation to share with me, so that I can share with others, a one- to two-minute video of active learning going on in your classroom, like this one-minute video of a Torts I class doing application exercises.

We usually look for evidence of learning in assessment scores, grade points, and bar passage, which are sound but to some degree indirect or at least later measures. A lot of variables, over and above your instruction, contribute to those outcomes. Yet we should be able to see direct evidence of learning going on in the engaged classroom. That's the point: to make learning visible so as to confirm, support, and enhance it.

If you can observe students learning in some form of engaged interaction with materials or others, then record it. Just use your cell phone to record the one- to two-minute video (anything longer gets unwieldy in file size). Then upload it to your Google Drive and share it with me. I will review it and, if appropriate, share it with the rest of us. Thank you, and enjoy the week.
Nelson

Enhancing Classroom Instruction No. 70: Please Reply to Me
[Assessment] [11/13/19]
Good morning, MBE-tested-course professors. Please reply to me with a few words about how your classroom work is going this term. I'd like to collect, make anonymous, and reflect back your replies, to encourage us in our community.

Classroom walls are isolating. Yet we tend to experience similar states of exultation, despair, joy, fear, elation, curiosity, weariness, satisfaction, and every other response across the spectrum, sometimes within a term and other times across terms.

As we struggle to first survive and then thrive, we alternately judge, blame, or credit ourselves, students, classes, generations, cultures, technologies, subjects, facilities, and many other variables.

Behind our responses, emotions, evaluations, judgments, behaviors, explanations, and justifications of why students are doing as they do are our commitments, values, insights, beliefs, assumptions, and presumptions.

We hear ourselves explain things to ourselves and sometimes to others. Let's take some solace, and maybe learn a thing or two from hearing one another. Please just reply with your first thought about how your term is going in the classroom. Anonymity assured.
Nelson

Enhancing Classroom Instruction No. 71: Communications Master File

[Resources] [11/14/19]

Good morning, MBE-tested-course professors. This email shares a link to a single, searchable, master file of all 71 of these daily messages that you have so far received over the past three months, with updated links to the resources and research to which the messages refer.

Please review and search this file to locate research, resources, templates, conversations, and recommendations that you recall may help you enhance instruction. I will keep this master file updated with each upcoming message.

We are together building and documenting valuable instructional expertise. No sense in losing track of our hard-won tools, insights, and methods. And remember that you also have a single table of the dates, numbers, titles, and description of each daily message. Thank you, and I hope you find something of help here.

Nelson

Enhancing Classroom Instruction No. 72: Conversation with Stevie Swanson

[Methods] [11/15/19]

Good morning, MBE-tested-course professors. Please consider listening to this conversation with our colleague Stevie Swanson about her latest efforts to enhance classroom instruction.

While Stevie shares many of her sound designs, some of her latest work entails an in-class pre-test over the day's topic followed by a later post-test over the same topic. Recall the studies showing that testing itself, the very act of working through a test, can have a powerful learning effect, even when students do not perform so well on the test. Stevie then uses the post-test results to further adjust her instruction, adding exercises or in-class review over topics on which students did not perform to standard.

Stevie knows the value of in-class engagement from her prior clinical-education instruction and, of course, from law practice. Her guiding principles are to make a safe place for students to venture, to strive, and to practice in class what they must perform on the bar exam and in practice. Listen to this conversation with Stevie to hear about many other sound designs by which she continues to reform her powerful instruction. Kudos to Stevie and to each of you who share her passion for student success.

Nelson

Enhancing Classroom Instruction No. 73: Prompt Midterm Feedback

[Assessment] [11/18/19]

Good morning, MBE-tested-course professors. Please consider our colleague Mary D'Isa's approach to scoring mid-term exams in a way that gives students prompt self-assessed feedback:

"For my Civ Pro midterm, I use the second half of class that week to go over the midterm--I actually make the students score their own exams (I make copies of their answer sheets so they cannot cheat)--and I put the Qs up on the screen one at a time and we go over every option and why the correct option is correct and why the incorrect options are wrong. Along the way, I try to instruct why certain options might be enticing but they are not the correct or best answer. I also ask students to tell me why when they get down to two choices and they chose the wrong option why they did. Their explanations, they readily admit, in hindsight are not very good. They gravitate to options that may repeat some of the facts or may state something that is true but not necessarily responsive to the call of the question. I have done this for several years now and get good feedback--they are usually too exhausted to concentrate on new material right after the midterm, and they like knowing so quickly how they did."

Notice not only that students get prompt feedback as they self-assess in rigorous fashion under Mary's guidance but that the practice also gives Mary feedback on why students are performing as they do. That feedback to the professor must help Mary adjust instruction, even as it helps one student see the pitfalls of other students.

Mary's method also considers students' social and emotional states, whether they are up to engaging new material. Kudos to Mary for her thoughtful design and for sharing it with us. Enjoy the week.

Nelson

Enhancing Classroom Instruction No. 74: Conversation with Mark Dotson
[Methods] [11/19/19]
Good morning, MBE-tested-course professors. Please consider listening to this conversation with our colleague Mark Dotson on classroom engagement.

Mark, as everyone knows, has the long teaching experience and deep practice insight to serve as a wise guide. In his comments, Mark emphasizes the importance of helping students read critically and then think through problems.

Drawing from his NITA and Trial Lawyers' College teaching experience, Mark engages students in the classroom in teams of judges, plaintiffs' lawyers, and defense lawyers, the judges examining the lawyers on their positions. Students learn to think critically.

We indeed must teach reading, reasoning, and advocacy skills, even as we help students learn substantial quantities of difficult doctrine. Mark has mastered social, professional, and identity aspects of learning that contribute substantially to student development.

Mark also has every student make an individual presentation to him, with instant feedback. Listen to a wise guide. And appreciate Mark's commitment and skill.
Nelson

Enhancing Classroom Instruction No. 75: Navigating Turbulence
[Morale] [11/20/19]
Good morning, MBE-tested-course professors. Please consider this suggestion about how to navigate institutional turbulence.

Rigorous instruction, whether lecturing, Socratic examination, or wider-engagement forms, is invigorating and satisfying but also mentally and physically draining. Reading dozens of hand-scrawled essay answers excites but strains the eyes. Concentrating for hours to assign fair and consistent exam scores, while writing hundreds of thoughtful, constructive, sensitive, and insightful comments, immerses but strains the mind. And doing these valuable things term after term year 'round, year after year, while an honor and privilege, can drain a restless imagination, test a divine spirit, and weary an aging soul.

Despite its odd rigors, this valuable work would largely remain a joy, not just a happy diversion, if the institutions within which one performs it were not at the same time presenting challenge after vexing challenge. Standards pile on standards, campuses open and close, media savages reputations, self-appointed prophets predict the institution's impending demise, and lawsuits fly, while scholars publish visions of the law profession's end. For anyone brave enough to poke one's head out of the classroom, disruption everywhere flies.

One helpful response can be to see that we are not alone in these sorts of apocalyptic challenges. You think being a law professor in this crazed environment is hard? Try being a retailer. Or a banker. Or an automaker. Or even an insurance salesperson. I had a meeting with professionals in those and other fields recently, in which each bemoaned what seemed to them like a tsunami of internal and external disruptions. Disruption is a sign of the times. Law school has always been a bellwether of sorts, for law itself is inherently social and political. No reason to feel more sorry for ourselves than for others.

But a more-helpful response may be that we still have the classroom, still have vital relationships with groups and classes of students. As professors, we must keep students as our first concern, shutting out the things that strive to distract us from treating those students as they deserve. I have the strong sense that when my time is over, whether sooner or later, I won't remember the programs, standards, and initiatives, won't remember the units, functions, departments, and committees. I will remember the students.

And so in yet another time of turbulence, I plan to focus on those students, shutting out the noise and distraction of a fearsome crowd. Join me, celebrating student relationships, in carefree faith, defying despair and defeat. Enjoy the week.
Nelson

Enhancing Classroom Instruction No. 76: How the Term Goes
[Assessment] [11/21/19]

Good morning, MBE-tested-course professors. Here for your interest is a link to a document with analyzed professor responses as to how the term is going for us.

Please review the responses. They document in fascinating detail many of the successes, challenges, celebrations, fears, innovations, frustrations, and other things we are all experiencing this term.

Take special note of the high frequency of instructional enhancements, indications of which I have highlighted. Collectively, we are on the move, having a sense of where we've been, where we are, and where we need to go. Read and review for those movements. Stasis we cannot accept. Movement we can.

Most of all, though, take heart that you are not alone in your commitments, efforts, questions, and concerns. Although we work independently and alone, we drive and thrive collectively, dependent on the initiative and insight of one another. Go, Team!
Nelson

Enhancing Classroom Instruction No. 77: Conversation with Tonya Krause-Phelan
[Methods] [11/22/19]
Good morning, MBE-tested-course professors. Please listen to this heartening conversation with our colleague Tonya Krause-Phelan about engaging students in the classroom.

We all know the passion with which Tonya, a NITA and Hillman instructor and first-rank defender, approaches a defense lawyer's precious craft. Tonya confirms in this conversation that her passion for sound criminal-justice advocacy drives her passion for effective instruction.

Clients charged with serious crimes, and governments constituted to charge them, need sound advocates that only a sound professional program can produce. After two decades of higher-education instruction, Tonya continues to find powerful new ways to marinate sound criminal law and procedure in strong advocacy skills instruction.

Tonya was a first adopter of WMU instructional-design-team support. This conversation shows some of the benefits she has drawn from that collaboration including several specific methods and activities that you might not have imagined, though once considered, seem so sound as to be obvious.

I hope you take the time to listen to this special conversation with another esteemed colleague wholly committed to outstanding instruction. Thank you, and enjoy the weekend.
Nelson

Enhancing Classroom Instruction No. 78: Conversation with Florise Neville-Ewell
[Methods] [11/25/19]
Good morning, MBE-tested-course professors. Please listen to this conversation with our esteemed colleague Florise Neville-Ewell on her multiple special enhancements supporting student learning.

You all know how committed Florise is to involving students in service work that helps them develop a professional persona. You may also know of the skills assessment that Florise has developed with the support of others to help students evaluate their learning needs. You may also have heard of how Florise ensures that students brief cases preparing for class, to increase the quality of class discussion and individual engagement.

What you may not know is the length to which Florise goes to help students prepare for mid-term and later essay assessments. Florise institutes a series of practice essays leading up to the essay mid-term. She scores those essays using a guide and shares the scoring and guide with students, individually and in group meetings outside of class hours, that she designs and conducts to enable students to incorporate critical feedback.

The depth, detail, and sensitivity that Florise shows in this assessment work is frankly remarkable, something well worth hearing and exploring. Listen also to the reason that Florise gives for the lengths to which she goes to support student learning. Appreciate the commitment of one very special colleague.
Nelson

Enhancing Classroom Instruction No. 79: Tammy Asher Class Recording
[Methods] [11/26/19]
Good morning, MBE-tested-course professors. A couple weeks ago, I asked anyone to share video of evidence of student learning in class. Our esteemed colleague Tammy Asher shared this fourteen-second video, worth your taking a quick look.

Notice from the video the high energy in the room, that all students are engaged in pairs with one another, that all students are working with structure (a paper or computer exercise), and that students are both speaking and reading or referring to sources.

Notice from the audio the snatches of law phrases that students are speaking and the serious professional tone with which students are communicating. All students appear to be on task, with good evidence that they are not only speaking but also listening to one another.

Give recording your class a try. If you find something interesting, then please share it with me so that I can evaluate it and share it with others. Our classrooms are dynamic places of learning. Let's collect more evidence of that dynamism.
Nelson

Enhancing Classroom Instruction No. 80: Why Improve Instruction
[Research] [11/27/19]
Good morning, MBE-tested-course professors. Think briefly, again, about why to improve instruction, drawn from research by a professor of psychology and education.

Accreditors want professional schools to select adversely for a certain group of "academically prepared" students who are already good at a certain standardized test that requires swift reading comprehension and logical reasoning. Yet as Columbia psychology professor Douglas Greer wrote in *The Teacher as Strategic Scientist*, the right methodology is instead to treat differences among students as auguring different instructional procedures. The question is not how certain populations perform under traditional instruction. We know that answer. The question is instead how instruction can produce mastery in each student, requiring that professors be strategically observant of student behavior.

Improving instruction justifies and energizes an access mission. If an access school can succeed with a student whom traditional schools cannot educate because of the traditional school's competitive rather than collaborative learning culture, imprecise and unscientific instructional methods, and lack of well-designed educational resources, then the access school will have fulfilled responsibly a role that traditional schools have not fulfilled. The access school will have qualified for the bar, against the same bar-exam admissions standard, a student whom traditional schools would not have qualified for the bar.

The access school would then be doing something both core (education) and important (democratic, uplifting, empowering, unifying, and diversifying) that traditional schools do not do. Precise, systematic instruction following evidence-based methods and principles can accomplish education's broader humanitarian goals. You are on the right path. Hew to it. And enjoy the Thanksgiving holiday.
Nelson

Enhancing Classroom Instruction No. 81: Why Traditional Instruction Fails
[Research] [12/02/19]
Good morning, MBE-tested-course professors. Consider how behavioral psychologist Jack Michael, in *The Essential Components of Effective Instruction and Why Most College Teaching Is Not*, summarizes how higher education, and by extension law school, tends in its traditional reading/lecture instructional format to fail students who need sound instruction.

First, the reading materials often lack the organization, prioritization, relevance demonstration, and other features and structure to adequately guide and inform students. Then, courses seldom specify for students the criteria for subject mastery, compounding the inadequacy of assigned materials. Without adequate instructional support, students naturally find competing contingencies from families, jobs, and other things that provide more immediate rewards than their opaque studies.

In behavioral terms, instruction offers poor control of the differential consequation for performing instructional tasks. Students initially study plenty but soon study too little, not because they are lazy but because of poor instructional design and poor control of differential consequation for studies. Differential consequation of correctness is also largely absent until the few, and usually final, exams. Students get too little formative feedback from which to diagnose errors and correct performance.

Especially for under-prepared students, the traditional program can be toxic. Let's continue to do a better job. And enjoy the week.
Nelson

Enhancing Classroom Instruction No. 82: Why Behavioral Approaches Help
[Research] [12/03/19]
Good morning, MBE-tested-course professors. Consider briefly why behavioral approaches to instruction, those strategies that focus on what students do, can be especially effective for under-performing students.

Behavioral approaches emphasize well-sequenced tasks of increasing difficulty, repeated practice in those tasks, feedback to correct performance, reinforcement to maintain correct performance, and frequent measurement to adjust instructional methods according to evidence-based practices.

Studies like those summarized in behavior analyst and special-education professor Cathy Watkins' *Project Follow Through*, show that these basic-skills approaches can help students gain more skills than traditional approaches, which can cause students to regress in basic skills. Evidence-based behavioral approaches prove their value.

Keep designing classroom environments that get students doing what you want them to do, which may largely be to recognize issues, recall and apply law, and analyze drawing on the complex goals of law. And enjoy the week.
Nelson

Enhancing Classroom Instruction No. 83: Generativity Theory
[Research] [12/04/19]

Good morning, MBE-tested-course professors. In your teaching, you may resist the cold hand of science as if it might discourage student creativity and your own creativity. Behavior analysts answer that resistance with generativity theory.

Psychology researcher Robert Epstein writes in *Cognition, Creativity, and Behavior* that creativity, like other behaviors, blends and alters old behaviors under new conditions. Creativity is not innate but a skill set, available to all.

One creative skill is to capture the fleeting thoughts that we all have every day, many of them subtle alterations, and a few of them profound alterations, of old thoughts. Those thoughts may never return, and so the creative thinker captures them. A second creative skill is to seek rather than avoid challenges. Challenges demand new combinations of old skills and solutions—demand, in other words, creativity.

A third skill is to place yourself in novel situations made up of strange events, objects, and people. Doing so requires modifying old behaviors into new combinations, broadening your skill base and deepening your generativity skill. A final skill is to keep learning new things, indeed, *anything new*. When you add new knowledge or skill, you multiply the creative solutions available to you from combining new with old knowledge and skills.

Creative people seem to have more with which to work because they do have more. But the more is not innate. Rather, acquire abundance through exploration. Explore teaching and learning like you've never explored them before. And enjoy the week.
Nelson

Enhancing Classroom Instruction No. 84: Kathy Gustafson Class Recording
[Methods] [12/05/19]
Good morning, MBE-tested-course professors. Please take forty-two seconds for this video of Kathy Gustafson's class engaged in their in-class exercises.

Note the larger class size and how Kathy has organized the students into natural pairs or three-somes. See how every student appears engaged.

Many students are talking, using their hands and expression dynamically, truly trying to communicate. Notice the listening students, too, who are not sitting mute and passive but are instead tracking their seatmate's talk closely, often nodding or interjecting to confirm or correct.

Above all, notice the class's high energy, which appears directed not to aimless argument or opinion in general but to addressing a problem that Kathy's exercises have posed. This video sure looks like evidence of learning. Impressive. Kudos to Kathy for her design and execution. And please keep the videos coming. Enjoy.
Nelson

Enhancing Classroom Instruction No. 85: Case-Briefing Template
[Resources] [12/06/19]
Good morning, MBE-tested-course professors. Please consider sharing with students Florise Neville-Ewell's case-briefing template available in her syllabus or in my modified form at this link and attached here.

Students can stumble over what information to glean from the many cases that we ask them to read. A template and guide like the one that Florise has developed, and for a time which she requires students to complete, can aid students in identifying priority information.

Please don't hesitate to share with me and others your own templates and guides. We can certainly exhort students in how to study, but templates and guides can also help them study with better effect. Thank you, and enjoy the weekend.
Nelson

Enhancing Classroom Instruction No. 86: Fading's Criticality
[Methods] [12/09/19]
Good morning, MBE-tested-course professors. Please consider how critical to instruction and learning is the little-known phenomenon of *fading*. Your instruction may be effective because of its presence or ineffective because of its absence, without your even realizing so.

Professors tend to focus greatly on the prompts like reading, lectures, slide shows, discussion, exercises, and testing, that reward students to gradually change behavior and thus "learn." Have you ever thought, though, of how you *remove* the prompts while trying to preserve the student behavior (what behavioral psychologists call *fading*)?

See, the answers are all in the book... and lecture, and Socratic examination, and elaborately prepared outlines, ... on and on. We flood students with prompts (presenting stimuli). How, though, are we transitioning students away from the prompts to performing without them? Traditional instruction goes straight from the full prompts to examination, setting up for failure those many students *who do not know how to fade.*

Skilled students know that they have to set aside the lecture and outline to practice their performance without them. That's what well-designed exercises do. They gradually move students from full-prompt, richly supported engagement, to engagement that triggers the shaped performance without prompt. To make an analogy of it, instruction should gradually wean students from the bottle until they are feeding themselves (performing without prompts). Consider whether and how your instruction does so. And enjoy the week.
Nelson

Enhancing Classroom Instruction No. 87: Designing Treatments
[Methods] [12/10/19]
Good morning, MBE-tested-course professors. Please consider the behavioral concept of *treatments* that may help you see more precisely what your instruction is doing.

Generally, professors offer substantial cues for learning. Readings, lectures, Socratic examination, slide shows, discussion, and testing all cue behaviors that professors must shape in students. Instruction in law, though, is more subtle than simply cuing students to *jump!* or *swing!* Behaviorists classify cues into three forms of what they call *treatments,* the three forms being *routine, shaping,* and *specialized* treatments. Treatments are the core of instruction.

Routine treatments involve explaining to students how to perform, giving examples of correct performance, stating rules and principles guiding performance, and then determining and implementing practice. Professors tend to be good at routine treatments.

Shaping treatments dissect performance into manageable units, focus on minimal responses, and adjust the type, quantity, and frequency of cuing (the routine treatments) to promote stronger responses. Professors tend to ignore shaping treatments, especially when they do not design, implement, and observe student practice. As a result, students may form study groups for shaping treatments or attempt the treatments on their own, however inexpertly. Consider whether your instruction offers shaping treatments.

Specialized treatments involve practicing incorrect responses until correct, backward chaining of steps to elicit correct responses, practice of principles before practice of the applicable procedure, and exaggerated stimuli or responses to clarify correct performance. Professors also tend to ignore specialized treatments, like they ignore shaping treatments. Students needing specialized treatments may rely on teaching assistants, academic-resource staff, or tutors. Your instruction can supply specialized treatments, reducing the need for others to do so.

I hope you see how subtle treatments are and how effective instruction offers a suitable range of them. Enjoy the week.
Nelson

Enhancing Classroom Instruction No. 88: Shaping Progressions
[Methods] [12/11/19]
Good morning, MBE-tested-course professors. Please consider a distinction in instruction, the difference between varying context and varying criteria, on which you may never have focused.

Students practice successive approximations toward the performance goal. No one expects them to perform perfectly initially. To induce improved performance, though, instruction must shape two variables, both the *context* in which the student must perform and the *criteria* for acceptable performance.

A simple task, such as to recognize the possibility of a fraud claim, can be difficult because of the many complex contexts (business sales, residential-home sales, investment opportunities) in which the task (identifying fraud) can arise. Simplifying context initially but then gradually making the context more complex is a context-dependent shaping strategy.

Other tasks are in themselves complex, even though the context may be simple or may vary little. Determining lien priority may be an example. Instruction can initially simplify performance criteria, requiring less of the task at once but then gradually increasing criteria toward the final performance, learning by successive approximation. For another example, professors may initially require students simply to organize an analysis in IRAC format but over time gradually require more-specific law/fact connections, stronger logic, and more-nuanced, balanced evaluations, as students advance in making those approximations.

These shaping progressions for achieving complex conceptual performances highlights the need for abundant designed practice with prompt feedback. The concept helps explain why engaged designs work, varying context and criteria, aiding approximations. I hope you find something helpful here. Enjoy the rest of the week.
Nelson

Enhancing Classroom Instruction No. 89: Engagement Dimensions
[Methods] [12/12/19]
Good morning, MBE-tested-course professors. Please consider three forms of in-class engagement that well-designed instruction supplies, in behavioral, cognitive, and relational dimensions.

The behavioral dimension requires students to participate with effort and persistence, following the designed activity's instructions in ways that advance learning. The behavioral dimension focuses on the quantity and outward appearance of student effort.

The cognitive dimension focuses on the quality of student effort, specifically the strategies and attitude that they deploy. A flurry of ineffective activity is not appropriate engagement. Some students seem to do a lot but accomplish little. Those students would lack cognitive engagement, the thoughtful, planned, self-managed, self-assessed, studied approach that produces learning rewards.

Relational engagement refers to the student's sense of instructor support, appropriate balance of interdependence and autonomy, belonging, confidence and trust in the classroom culture, and other emotional and affective factors influencing learning. Students may be cognitively and behaviorally engaged but unfortunately isolated, mistrustful, overly dependent on instructor support, or unduly competitive with classmates.

Engagement's three dimensions, behavioral, cognitive, and relational, should work together in integrated fashion, one supporting the other. Don't hesitate to disclose these dimensions to students, to set classroom expectations. Watch for and foster them--all three of them. And enjoy the end of the week.
Nelson

Enhancing Classroom Instruction No. 90: End-of-Term Congratulations
[Morale] [12/13/19]
Good morning, MBE-tested-course professors. We have together made it to term's end. Congratulations on another one in the figurative and literal books. Thank you for persevering through these messages, reflecting together on our instruction. With your permission, or to your relief, the messages will now cease until next term, giving us a well-earned break.

Best wishes that students perform well on your final exams. My hope is that you see stronger student work from top to bottom, that higher-performing students perform even higher while lower-performing students do not perform so low. We begin anew with students every term, meaning that enhancement in instruction can only be incremental. We build from the foundation up every term, hoping only to build with greater insight and skill.

Please continue, over the break and beyond, to share with me your instructional insights. You have opened my eyes to much more of your good work this term. And please let me know if you think instructional enhancement can move in other directions, whether in assessing our practices or deploying additional methods. I have a nagging sense, maybe one that you share, of having only scratched the surface, when also sensing that time is short. Wring from the time its complete richness. And enjoy the Christmas and New Year's holiday.
Nelson

Enhancing Classroom Instruction No. 91: Preparing a Flipped Lecture
[Methods] [01/06/20]
Good morning, MBE-tested-course professors, and welcome back from break. In the schoolwide initiative to engage more students more fully in class, please consider these suggestions on preparing a flipped lecture.

The flipped classroom swaps in-class mostly passive presenting stimuli like lectures and slideshows to online forums outside the classroom, so that students when gathered in the classroom can benefit from one another's presence and the professor's presence. Students can watch and listen to lectures online, while they cannot as readily engage one another and their professor online, which is instead the unusual benefit of the classroom.

How, though, does one prepare a flipped lecture? Consider making a copy of your in-class slideshow, preserving the original for use in class if and when you continue in-class lecture and discussion. Then pare down the outside-of-class copy of your in-class slideshow to its law essentials. If your original slideshow was twenty or thirty slides, highlighting cases and policy and arguments, then force yourself to winnow slides to from five to ten.

The goal is to reduce and refine the information to very clearly organized and formatted slides that you can narrate in no more than about twenty minutes. Concentration wanes beyond that length. Then, animate each slide so that the information that you are reading and interpreting for students is the only new information appearing on the slide. You can also use the pointer (enlarge your cursor) to point out the information that you are highlighting as you narrate.

More detail next time on how to record, download, and post to Canvas a flipped lecture. Fine alternatives exist. The point is to practice and refine flipped lectures until you have weekly videos that students can readily access, follow, and digest before class. Enjoy the week and term.
Nelson

Enhancing Classroom Instruction No. 92: Recording a Flipped Lecture
[Methods] [01/07/20]

Good morning, MBE-tested-course professors. Yesterday's message suggested how to prepare a flipped, outside-of-class lecture so that students come to class prepared to actively engage the week's topic.

Remember that flipped lectures allow students to view your lecture on their own, shifted time, while using class, when students are together, for activities that require students to be together. Makes sense, doesn't it? The law school's partner WMed does not allow professors to gather students in class only to lecture, when students could instead watch lectures online to make better use of precious, gathered, class time.

So, to record a lecture, consider using your WebEx account to record your animated lecture, download it, and upload it to your Canvas page for posting as a weekly resource. Turn on your prepared slideshow, sign in to WebEx, start a meeting, choose audio but no video, then choose the shared-presentation screen to show your computer screen. When ready, hit record. Lecture through your slideshow, hitting pause (then resume) whenever you need any break. End the recording, and end the meeting.

WebEx can take up to a few hours to process your recording, depending on its length. Initially, it may not appear at all on your WebEx recordings page. Don't fret. It should show up later in the day or the next day. Check your WebEx recordings page. When it appears, feel free to rename it to something identifiable like "Evidence Week 1 Summary Recording," using the options button on the recording's line, to the far right of the screen.

Make a few of these flipped lectures, and you'll be a total pro. I've made dozens of them for several courses, with increasing facility. The first time is hard, second not so much, third a charm. Tomorrow's message will give tips on how to post the flipped lecture to your Canvas course page. Enjoy the week.
Nelson

Enhancing Classroom Instruction No. 93: Posting a Flipped Lecture to Canvas
[Methods] [01/08/20]
Good morning, MBE-tested-course professors. Yesterday's message suggested how to record a flipped, outside-of-class lecture using WebEx,

so that students who view it can come to class prepared to actively engage the week's topic.

To get the completed recording on your Canvas course page, go back to your WebEx account, choose the recordings screen, locate the recording you just made (remember that WebEx may take a few hours to process your recording, depending on its length), and download it to your computer. Then go to your Canvas course, choose the files page, choose upload, and go to your computer download folder to choose and upload to Canvas the recording you just made. Then go to your Canvas course's modules page, scroll to the module (I make my modules in weeks, as many of you do) where you want to post the lecture, and click the + button to add the recording to the module. The menu starts with Assignments, so drop that option down to the Files option to find your just-uploaded recording.

Once you upload the flipped recording to your chosen module (week), you can rename it and move it around within the module. I put my flipped recordings first in my modules (a separate module for each week) so that students encounter it first and are more likely to watch it, perhaps even before doing the week's reading but surely before class. Students should come to class better prepared for engaged activities. I hope these explanations have helped. Enjoy the week.
Nelson

Enhancing Classroom Instruction No. 94: Spectacular Review Method
[Methods] [01/09/20]
Good morning, MBE-tested-course professors. With apologies for my hyperbole, please consider watching two brief videos of a very special review method that our colleague Kim O'Leary used in her Review Week class last term.

The first video shows students gathering around large sheets of paper that Kim has on the classroom walls, to collaboratively record a course outline from memory. Kim writes topics at the top of each sheet for students to fill in from memory. Notice the very high level of engagement on task.

73

The second video shows more detail of the outline sheets as students fill them in. Kim requires students to bring their outlines to class but does not permit them to bring their outlines up to the wall to write on the sheets. Kim reviews the collaborative outline, completed in about forty minutes, for accuracy and completeness, permitting students to take photos of the collaborative outline, as many do.

This active method still left Kim two hours for other review, which she spent this past term on students working essays. Kim did an outstanding job not only in designing this activity but also in recording it. Please watch video 1 and video 2. They are, well, spectacular in inspiration--no hyperbole. Enjoy the last of the week.
Nelson

Enhancing Classroom Instruction No. 95: Sequencing Engagement
[Methods] [01/10/20]
Good morning, MBE-tested-course professors. Please consider a helpful insight from our colleague Kim O'Leary related to message No. 89 late last term. That message suggested that effective in-class engagement involves behavioral, cognitive, and relational dimensions. Here's Kim:

"One thing I learned at a session at the Denver conference (Online and Hybrid learning) this September was that research shows that if you provide more structured guidance early in a course, this fosters more independence later in the course. [Many] think it's all or nothing - structured guidance or autonomous learning, but there is a sequence."

Kim's insight suggests that your in-class designs should change across the term, perhaps moving from more behavioral and relational dimensions toward more cognitive dimensions, and definitely moving from simpler, more-foundational exercises to more-complex and creative problem solving.

I suspect that you've observed the same phenomenon in your in-class exercises, that after a few early weeks of practicing behaviors and building relationships, students are ready to take on ever-more-complex problems, applying progressively linked, complex protocols using honed skills.

Thank you again to Kim for this insight. If you have observed something like this phenomenon, please don't hesitate to share it with me for sharing with others. Enjoy the weekend.
Nelson

Enhancing Classroom Instruction No. 96: Producing Workbooks
[Resources] [01/13/20]
Good morning, MBE-tested-course professors. Please consider again whether colleagues also teaching your course and I might help you prepare an organized workbook offering staged in-class exercises for each week of the term.

Late last term, our colleague Erika Breitfeld and I developed this draft of a nearly three-hundred-page Criminal Law workbook, which Erika plans now to revise in use through this term and supplement with other exercises she develops and Tonya and other colleagues contribute. Erika and I may soon publish the workbook in paperback format, but until then she makes it available to students as a coursepack, pdf file, and Word file.

This Criminal Law workbook joins similar workbooks for Torts I, Torts II, and Property I, in use at the law school. Handouts work well for in-class engagement. Workbooks can significantly simplify and streamline the process, relieving you of a lot of copying and passing out paper, and enabling you to switch activities on the fly. Please let me know if you're interested in having a workbook. And enjoy the week.
Nelson
P.S. Congratulate Erika on her innovation and perseverance in bringing about this work.

Enhancing Classroom Instruction No. 97: Student Insights on Learning
[Assessment] [01/14/20]
Good morning, MBE-tested-course professors. Please accept this invitation to solicit, collect, and share with me student insights on learning.

Students don't always know what's good for them. Students can be especially misguided when mistaking for wasted time, the kind of effortful striving necessary for learning. Working in the zone of proximal development, where learning takes place, can be emotionally, psychologically, and even physically uncomfortable, which students can overlook.

Students can also be misguided when mistaking the illusion of knowledge, that natural ease that comes with listening to a polished lecture and recognizing terms, for deep learning that enables a student to apply those terms. Deep learning wrestling with concept distinction, application, and analysis can be uncomfortable, which students may try to avoid.

Yet students can also discern things about their learning that can confirm, correct, or otherwise guide our instruction. The key here is not to look for general student affirmation but instead for student insight into why certain strategies, activities, and resources work, especially when we can see the principles on which that success draws. Students can be remarkable in their insights, especially when trained in education, as some are.

So please consider soliciting student views, either from your whole class or from individual students whose discernment you recognize and respect. Share those insights with me, and I will share them with the group of us. Thank you, and enjoy the week.
Nelson

Enhancing Classroom Instruction No. 98: Professor Insights on Students
[Assessment] [01/15/20]
Good morning, MBE-tested-course professors. Please accept this email inviting your summary of specific student experiences reflecting their deployment of successful learning strategies demonstrating deeper principles of learning.

Here's the idea. We each witness student marvels, those miracles in which students with rudimentary writing and articulation skills, and average or below-average academic records, overcome their shortcomings to perform admirably well or better, even outstandingly well.

These students may especially be the ones who go on to become great practitioners, not full of themselves and their accomplishments, because their accomplishments are ordinary, but full of the attitude that with the right preparation and execution, they can weave gold from straw, meaning perhaps to save a business, win a tough civil-rights case, settle a nasty dispute, and so on.

When you remember one of those students, or find the next one, please share with me the insight that you gleaned from them, or they shared with you, about their learning. They may not even know why they did better than predicted, but you may know or be able to figure it out. Share with me so that I can share with others. Thank you, and enjoy the week.
Nelson

Enhancing Classroom Instruction No. 99: Ode to Professing
[Morale] [01/16/20]
Good morning, MBE-tested-course professors. In sure hands (not mine), poetry can open the soul to hidden emotions and inspiration, so please accept for general encouragement this ode to teaching law:

> No more scoffing at feared law profs
>   Who having honed the subtle craft
> No longer infamy's halls haunt
>   But find no student quite so daft
>
> As unable law sure to learn
>   To pass the bar, license follow,
> Profession livelihood to earn,
>   No matter friv'lous or hollow,
>
> Hero 'stead client eyes beheld,
>   For standing sure and bold in fray,
> Bills paid, justice done, coffers swelled
>   'Nough student loans easily pay.

Apologies to all, but sometimes one has to see both the profound and humorous in one's own craft. Please consider sharing with me, for broader sharing, your own ode to law teaching, indeed a subtle but rich craft. Enjoy the week.
Nelson

Enhancing Classroom Instruction No. 100: Metaphors as Obstacles
[Research] [01/17/20]
Good morning, MBE-tested-course professors. Please consider how the metaphors that we naturally use for teaching and learning can become obstacles to enhancing instruction.

We are all well aware of older, mechanistic metaphors for thinking and learning, characterized by the image (reproduced below) of gears inside one's head. We know, to the contrary, that health, social relations, emotions, and other things affect thinking and learning, beyond its mechanistic nature, making the metaphor potentially misleading.

Newer metaphors, characterized as *brain science*, replace the old mechanistic gear image with electrical and physiological images that are no more helpful, or not much more helpful, than the old gears. The new images tell us little to nothing more of what students are doing when thinking and learning.

The most-misleading images, though, may be ones that the teaching profession generally and law school specifically have employed. One of those images is of knowledge poured into the student brain as container. When we speak of the importance of "coverage," we are probably referring to this metaphor, that we must pour out or *cover* critical topics in lecture, slideshow, or other stimulus.

Consider carefully the metaphors that you accept and use on which to base instruction. I prefer behavioral terms, which attempt to reduce or eliminate metaphors altogether for student performance. We understand the world through metaphor, as George Lakoff writes in *Metaphors We Live By*. Choose metaphors carefully. Enjoy the weekend.
Nelson

Enhancing Classroom Instruction No. 101: Metaphors as Tools
[Research] [01/20/20]
Good morning, MBE-tested-course professors. Please consider how metaphor can be not only an obstacle to enhanced instruction but also a tool.

George Lakoff and Mark Johnson in the 1980 classic *Metaphors We Live By* suggested that metaphors draw from a source domain, the things we know by experience, to project onto the target domain, the thing we are trying to understand. Metaphor helps us reason using our experience, analogic rather than analytic reasoning, as professionals tend to practice, drawing from experience. The key to drawing more-powerful metaphors is first to recognize the source lens through which we view the target subject. Does that lens make sense, meaning the lens attributes equate to critical attributes of the target subject? Or are the lens attributes false equivalents, misleading as to the target's nature? The next step to drawing more-powerful metaphors is to propose alternatives.

Consider again the popular concept that when a professor covers (lectures about, represents in a slideshow, includes in an outline, etc.) a topic, students have learned it or will learn it. Covering focuses on inputs, things the professor offers or does. Covering does not focus on performances or outcomes, things the student does. The attributes of covering as a metaphor for learning or instruction thus do not equate well with what learning entails, which is to change one's behavior in a way that endures after instruction.

Perhaps, then, learning's better metaphor is driving a car, something about which one can certainly hear or read (inputs) but that is very different from those inputs in that it requires doing, action, practice, trial and error under safe circumstances until meeting a road test. Remember driver's ed? Instruction took only a day or two to put the student on the literal road. Learning law may be far more intellectual than driving, which we tend to think of as involving primarily motor skill, but it still requires physical performance (selection, writing, sometimes more) responding to complex stimuli, not entirely different than knowing the rules of the road. Explore your teaching-and-learning metaphor, to select the best understanding tool. And enjoy the week.
Nelson

Enhancing Classroom Instruction No. 102: Student Profile
[Assessment] [01/21/20]
Good morning, MBE-tested-course professors. A few days ago, I invited any of you to share the profile of a student whom you saw using specific strategies to unusually good effect, demonstrating learning principles. Here is an example.

A student had pretty much led the student's class throughout law school, hard working, brilliant, mature, disciplined, and enormously insightful. Bar passage was no issue. The cost of a bar-prep course, though, was an issue. This student had no other support, wasn't going to borrow, and had worked at least part-time throughout. So, the student decided to forgo a bar-prep course, which was fine because the student had every ability and discipline necessary to pass easily.

The question, though, was what bar-prep strategy the student, now a graduate, would employ. The graduate's study practices had been traditional: reading, re-reading, outlining, and paying attention while taking good notes in class. Yet the graduate wasn't going to leave bar-prep to traditional study forms. The graduate felt a need to disaggregate the graduate's learning, turn the whole bodies of law learned into discrete rules for quick recall and accurate application.

And so, the graduate made an enormous stack of flashcards, maybe six hundred of them. This student was probably the least likely to believe in flashcards during law school. No one was using them much, no professor touting them, when the student went through. The student already knew how to learn vast quantities of rules simply from traditional study forms and, more than that, had a most-highly developed sense of how the world works and should work.

Yet the student chose flashcards, and of course, they worked. Another graduate, the student's law school nemesis, had challenged the student to see who would score the highest on the bar exam. The two scored higher than any other graduate from that class, just one point separating them. One had paid for a commercial bar-prep course. The other, the flashcard user, had not. Sound strategies, applied with discipline and sound resources, work. I hope you find something encouraging in this profile. Enjoy the week.
Nelson

Enhancing Classroom Instruction No. 103: Using Canvas Studio
[Methods] [01/22/20]
Good morning, MBE-tested-course professors. Here are Lauren's helpful tips on using Canvas Studio instead of WebEx to record your flipped lectures, likely a preferred tool:

"I am doing the flipped lecture approach in my classes this term. ... I've tried to keep the videos relative short and focused on a narrow part of any given topic. For example, I have created six videos for Subject Matter Jurisdiction - one containing some general introductory info, two on diversity, one on fed Q, one on Supplemental Jdx, and one on removal.

"... I am using Canvas Studio, in 'Screen Capture' mode. This allows me to record the PowerPoint slides that I made for the lecture, and I appear (as a talking head) in the lower right corner of the screen. One of the great things about using Studio is I can embed quiz questions right in the video - multiple choice, true/false, and multiple answer. I've embedded several quiz questions in most of the videos. Once you finish recording the video, it uploads and 'finishes' within only a few minutes, and you can post it to your Canvas page right away.

"Taught my first class yesterday using this approach - I had posted three videos to the Class 1 module, totaling not quite an hour of lecture, and added some cool new exercises to my class time, including a hypo that required students to read and apply a section of the US Constitution, 28 USC 1332(a), and FRCP 12(b). The point of the exercise was to get students reading the procedural 'positive law' right from the source, and to demonstrate how the different 'layers' of procedural law fit together.

"Overall, I think the re-make of my Civ Pro I class using the video lectures went well. We'll see how it goes in future classes!"

How is your flipping going? Please feel free to share your thoughts with me for circulation to others. And enjoy the rest of the week.
Nelson

Enhancing Classroom Instruction No. 104: The Classroom's Significance
[Methods] [01/23/20]
Good morning, MBE-tested-course professors. Please consider this brief note about the classroom's continuing significance to learning.

Classrooms are fast becoming peculiar places. Education increasingly relies on online synchronous or even asynchronous instructional delivery, where students gather only virtually if even that, and on labs, clinics, and field placements.

On-the-job training, technology-based training, e-learning whether instructor or student led, and job performance aids can all be reasonable alternatives, and in many cases preferred alternatives, to classroom instruction.

Yet for us, classrooms remain the delivery locus for first-year and second-year instruction. Classrooms thus have an outsized influence on law-student performance. What happens or doesn't happen in the classroom still matters to law students.

Classrooms are also increasingly rare communities, in a society that relies ever more on social media and other virtual stimulation for the associations, affinities, and relationships that characterize American life.

Classrooms should thus especially promote healthy, positive, constructive, and equitable relationships, not just between professors and students but also among students. Get the classroom right, and you do students a great service. Keep at your good classroom work.
Nelson

Enhancing Classroom Instruction No. 105: Student Self-Regulation
[Methods] [01/24/20]
Good morning, MBE-tested-course professors. Please consider this brief note of the role of student self-regulation in learning, and how to foster it.

Well-designed classroom engagement promotes student self-regulation by shifting regulation's locus from professor to student. Engagement designs remove you from the enforcer role in favor of a guide role that helps students frame their self-regulation.

First, set expectations for classroom engagement to help students adjust and plan their behaviors. Require students to partner, but let students select partners, change partners within an exercise and across classes, and choose and adjust group size.

Next, help students set engagement goals, like, "Let's work through these first two exercises in ten minutes before reporting out answers," but then let students take more or less time as they are able or require, planning next exercises for those who finish early.

Then, monitor performance phases. Do not leave the classroom or do email or other work. Attend fully to how students are engaging and performing. Use mini-interventions as you perceive the need, not as an enforcer but to remind of expectations, highlight especially effective work, or clarify instructions.

End engagement with reflection in which students share insights. Reflection can be from you to the class, from individual students to the class, or between new pairs and groups of students in rearranged fashion. Reflection promotes accountability. Use these and other methods to foster self-regulated, self-directed classroom learning. And enjoy the weekend.
Nelson

Enhancing Classroom Instruction No. 106: Fixed and Variable Consequences
[Research] [01/27/20]
Good morning, MBE-tested-course professors. Here's a brief note about fixed and variable consequences that may relieve some of your anxiety over effectively influencing student behavior.

Instructors rely on antecedent (prior) stimuli, like an exhortation to "Do this!" or a demonstration of the behavior, say, working out a problem on the whiteboard before asking students to do so. Clear, helpful, consistent antecedents aid learning. Yet instructors also rely on consequences to behavior, in the long view grades and bar passage or failure, and in the short view scores, credit, admonishments ("Come see me in my office!") and praise. Consequences are also important to learning.

Not surprisingly, short-term consequences can affect learning more than long-term consequences. Both you and the student can see that the student is going to fail the bar if continuing down the student's current path. But the short-term consequences don't sufficiently influence more-effective studies, and so the student persists down the path. A more-interesting feature of consequences is, though, that they need not be fixed, ever-present, always supplied. They can instead be more effective when variable. Variable does not mean unfair, inconsistent, contradictory. Variable just means sometimes present while sometimes not present.

So, don't worry that you praise sometimes but not others, or score sometimes and not others, or admonish sometimes but not others. Instead, supply consequences strategically, variably, when you can, when students expect them and when they do not expect them. Varying the consequences can promote self-regulated learning, like a pat on the back sometimes but not all the time. I hope you see something helpful here. Enjoy the week.
Nelson

Enhancing Classroom Instruction No. 107: Student Feedback on Engagement
[Assessment] [01/28/20]
Good morning, MBE-tested-course professors. A couple of weeks ago, I encouraged you to solicit and share student feedback on learning. Here's a guiding and confirming comment our colleague Kim O'Leary received:

"[M]y Property II students from M-2019 got really high grades, as a group. I bumped into a student, before grades were released (last week) and she asked, 'How'd we do?' I told her that I didn't know who got what grade, but as a group, the grades were incredibly high. She said, 'That's because you made us work together!'"

High grades hearten. Positive student comments about techniques and culture also hearten. But also notice that the student asked how "we" did, which in itself is an indication that students viewed their efforts in Kim's course as a collective, collaborative, rather than competitive, effort. Kudos to Kim for building in engagement.
Nelson

Enhancing Classroom Instruction No. 108: What Is Knowledge?
[Research] [01/29/20]
Good morning, MBE-tested-course professors. Please give a moment's thought to something foundational: the meaning or nature of knowledge. Instruction fails when misconceiving the deep nature of knowledge as a

commodity, a thing to acquire and possess. Knowledge, as some ancients and fewer moderns properly conceive it, is instead relational: we know by being known.

The professor's guru Parker Palmer, who wrote the best-seller *The Courage to Teach*, first wrote a smaller but better book *To Know as We Are Known*. The book, the title of which refers to a verse in Paul's love chapter 1 Corinthians 13, confirms the relational basis not only of teaching but of the knowledge that the teacher hopes to impart. Effective teachers simply mediate between knower and unknown.

For lawyers especially, knowledge is valuable, indeed knowledge exists, only insofar as it enables others to see, hear, and come alongside the lawyer, that is, for others to know the lawyer. The power of a lawyer lies not in the arrangement of words but in the presence that the words convey, the presence of truth, and not truth as theory or object but as a person, perhaps the lawyer or maybe someone larger whom the lawyer inhabits.

We have each had a sense of knowledge's depth, purity, and power to move, those classroom moments when its presence shatters ignorance and indolence, moving even the immovable student to insight expressed in revelation. Phil Prygoski used to refer to them as those "whooo" moments for which one plans, strives, strains, and reaches every class, every term, but instead appear on their own, perhaps only when we prostrate ourselves before them. Don't underestimate knowledge. Enjoy the rest of the week.
Nelson

Enhancing Classroom Instruction No. 109: Shaping Contingencies
[Research] [01/30/20]
Good morning, MBE-tested-course professors. Please consider this abstract of the attached seminal B.F. Skinner article on *The Science of Learning and Art of Teaching*. Skinner, you'll recall, is the grandfather of behavior analysis who showed you could teach pigeons to play ping pong and who (to a degree) raised his infants in a carefully controlled box.

The attached article confirms that by progressively changing contingent reinforcements, one can achieve instruction in extremely complex performances. That gradual shaping of contingencies is what effective instruction does. One need then only continue the contingencies long enough to confirm the learned behavior, which is the spacing and repetition to which memory advocates refer.

While Skinner initially used non-human animals as a basis for study, he did so to isolate and simplify our gross complexities, to address our attention, problem solving, self-control, and other response systems. The key is to identify and sequence scheduled responses..., that when the environment presents one stimulus, the student should respond one way, and another stimulus, a different way.

Response sequencing is why our instruction should vary variables as it leads students through consistent responses to our concepts' critical attributes. See how Skinner describes classroom instruction as it moved from primarily aversive controls to more-effective reinforcements--the same pattern followed in law schools as they reformed their previously aversive instruction.

See, too, how important Skinner regards the skillful programming of sequenced reinforcements. Here is where we have much work to do. Examine the notes and problems in your casebook, and you are likely to find jumbles of mostly unanswered, ambiguous, boundary questions that fascinate skilled professors, when students instead need more rehearsal of the core concepts.

I hope you find something inspirational in Skinner's clear, groundbreaking writing and his close, scientific critique of the modern classroom's shortcomings. He describes the very journey on which we have embarked over the past decade in enhancing instruction. Enjoy the rest of the week.
Nelson

Enhancing Classroom Instruction No. 110: The Latest in Behavioral Instruction
[Research] [01/31/20]
Good morning, MBE-tested-course professors. Please consider this abstract of the attached article by Kent Johnson on *Behavioral Education in the 21st Century*. The article recognizes that the current challenge isn't

so much knowledge acquisition as developing real-world skills, a goal dear to this law school.

Dr. Johnson, a director of the groundbreaking Morningside Academy, addresses how to make the flipped classroom more generative and engaging, with activity-driven instruction improving social interaction, thinking, reasoning, and problem-solving skills. Behavior analysis first focused on organizing and managing the classroom to increase instructional time. It now focuses on the quality of that instructional time.

Dr. Johnson identifies *generativity* as a goal of instruction. Instruction cannot possibly teach students all they need to know and do. It must instead teach behaviors that can generate or produce knowledge and actions fitting to new circumstances. Dr. Johnson recommends teaching generative repertoires like questioning diagramming, thinking through interacting, and organizational repertoires.

I teach and use in class the Think Aloud Paired Problem-Solving (TAPPS) method Dr. Johnson recommends. Keep sharing those high-value, generative repertoires. Move toward an activity-driven classroom that builds generativity. And enjoy the weekend.
Nelson
P.S. By the way, my WMU grad assistant Kyle Kenny shared the chapter yesterday and article today, one of the several great benefits of working with the WMU grad team.

Enhancing Classroom Instruction No. 111: Planning Assessment
[Assessment] [02/03/20]
Good morning, professors. Here, early in the term, just after finishing last term's grading, consider just how complex and technical assessment is—the most-complex function professors undertake. And reconsider whether your assessment is accomplishing what you set out for it to do.

Professors Brown and Green in *Essentials of Instructional Design* discern that assessment begins when you identify its purpose, of which one can have several including certifying (licensing), winnowing (advancement), rewarding (scholarship), evaluating (planning further instruction), shaping (formative assessment), or satisfying institutional or accreditation mandates (compliance). Recognize your purposes, and share with examinees those purposes.

Next, confirm which students take the test. Some may not need to do so, while others may not be ready to do so. Then, judge how much time to devote the test and who will administer it under what conditions. Next, confirm the knowledge and skills that the test will address, confirming the nature and scope of the test content. hen decide on the test-item format or formats and the number of items for each format. Also, confirm whether you may or must draw items from a pool and whether you may or must draft additional items.

Then determine the item difficulty including the taxonomy level, whether recall, comprehension, application, analysis, synthesis, or evaluation. Next, develop the sequence of test items, which in itself may affect performance. Then, determine the scoring method. In the process, determine if and how you will communicate feedback to students. Finally, consider whether you will have item analyses performed for difficulty and discrimination, and whether you will assess reliability and measurement error.

Do not underestimate the value, sensitivity, complexity, and technicality of assessment. Following these steps ensures that you give appropriate attention to what is both a surprisingly complex while also obviously important procedure. Reevaluate if you have the right assessment purposes, format, method, and mix. Start early, preparing your assessments. Consider drafting assessments before preparing instruction. And enjoy the emerging new term.
Nelson

Enhancing Classroom Instruction No. 112: Four Types of Assessment Decision
[Assessment] [02/04/20]
Good morning, professors. We do well in planning assessment to keep in mind the decisions that we make, and students make, based on assessment. Consider the four types of decisions that Professor Hosp articulated in his chapter *Using Assessment Data to Make Decisions.*

First, both professors and students use assessments for *screening* decisions when planning instruction, courses, and curriculum. A student may use early assessment results to drop the course, while a professor may use the same result to coach the student or direct the student to other resources. Screening assessments presume predictive power. The professor should have validated results to performance goals.

Professors also use assessments for *progress* decisions. Progress assessments are formative in nature, benchmarking student performance to standards approaching the performance goal. Unlike screening assessments, progress assessments require feedback mechanisms, enough so that the professor can adjust instruction and students can adjust performance. Be sure that your progress assessments supply adequate feedback.

Other assessments enable *diagnostic* decisions. Diagnostic assessments may contain greater detail, enabling the professor to discern student knowledge errors or method errors. Diagnostic assessments allow professors to adjust instruction to reduce collective error rates and to reach individual students needing study, skill, and performance adjustments. Be sure that you are implementing those adjustments as your assessments show collective and individual error rates.

Other assessments, especially final exams, enable *outcome* decisions having to do with student and professor accountability to performance goals and institutional standards. Outcome assessments should alignment not only to instruction but also to instructional and institutional standards. Are we each performing as well as we should, and are students meeting institutional standards? Keep in mind these four decisions when designing and implementing your assessment. And enjoy the week.
Nelson

Enhancing Classroom Instruction No. 113: Assessment Narratives
[Assessment] [02/05/20]
Good morning, professors. You may have recently finished scoring dozens of essay-exam answers or other papers. What can we learn from a close examination of your experience?

Below for your consideration is a typical scoring narrative. Please consider sharing with me your own narrative, as authentic and revealing as you can make it. And enjoy the week.

Nelson

The professor opened another copy of the electronic scoring rubric, entered the next student's exam number, confirmed that the student had correctly answered all ten multiple-choice questions, and then began reading the essay answer, preparing to complete the scoring rubric. The exam was the thirtieth that the professor had already graded that afternoon, but already the student's issue statement had captured the professor's admiration. He promptly checked the three mastery-level benchmarks for issue statements on the electronic rubric form. The student's rule section was modest, but the professor read on, hoping to see more law worked into the analysis. A lengthy and balanced analysis followed, indeed picking up several subsidiary rules that the student had initially omitted from the rule section. The answer ended with a clear, evaluative, and sound conclusion. The professor, duly impressed, checked mastery boxes right down the line on the electronic form. Then, he typed several superlatives, each tied to a specific part of the answer, in the form's comment box before pausing and just managing, with a silent smile, to craft something constructively critical. The professor ended the comments with a big *Thank you!* Finally, for good measure, the professor typed *Go straight to graduation!* hoping that the second-term student would appreciate the encouraging humor.

Enhancing Classroom Instruction No. 114: Assessment Measurement
[Methods] [02/06/20]
Good morning, professors. You may have recently completed scoring dozens of essay answers or other papers, perhaps wondering (as we all do from time to time) whether your measurements were sound. Please consider again three dimensions and two tools of sound assessment measurement, after first considering scoring's objective.

Measurement should equate a range of equivalent unit numbers to the range of student performances aiming toward the learning goal. One student should receive the same score as another student who performs to the same standard, with the numeric scores also equating among relative performances, higher scores for stronger performances and lower scores for weaker performances.

Given that scoring objective, measurement must meet three criteria: (1) accuracy; (2) validity; and (3) reliability. Your measurement must assign the performance's true value (accuracy), assign a score to the performance that your assessment intended to measure (validity), and assign scores consistently over time, unaffected by other factors outside of the student's performance (reliability).

Selecting what to measure and score, aligned to the performance goal supported by instruction, is critical to effective assessment. Two tools help that measurement: (1) clear definitions of the target behavior, reflected in model answers; and (2) systematic observational schemes like those in well-developed scoring rubrics. You cannot measure what you cannot define.

Measurement is key to the quality, fairness, and effectiveness of our instructional efforts. Keep in mind measurement's three dimensions, and use sound measurement tools, both model answers and scoring rubrics. And enjoy the week.
Nelson

Enhancing Classroom Instruction No. 115: Measurement Versus Diagnosis
[Assessment] [02/07/20]
Good morning, professors. As you prepare again to score papers and exams, please consider an important (indeed obvious but still-helpful) distinction between criterion measurement and performance diagnosis.

A first step in scoring is to measure student performance against the criterion, determining whether the student met the performance objective. Importantly, in doing so, you are not determining *why* the student met the objective or failed to meet the objective. You are simply measuring performance against standard. A model answer and well-developed scoring rubric help your scoring accuracy, validity, and reliability.

Diagnosing *why* the student performed or failed to perform requires a different set of test items or observations. For instance, a failing student may have acquired the knowledge and skill but not had the available time, tools, or resources, or been distracted or ill. Conversely, a passing student may have guessed, or you may have chosen the one topic for which the student had managed to prepare. Passing or failing performance is simply a measurement, not a diagnosis.

Effort and attitude are not always the diagnosis for passing or failing. A hard-working student might have failed to meet a scholarly paper's criteria because the student did not have access to the research database or word processor, or had other assignments or illness interfere, despite having the discipline and skill to succeed. Student can also fail because instruction does not point them toward the required performances in precise, structured, and rewarding manner, leaving them without knowledge and skill.

Take an interest not only in criterion measurement but also performance diagnosis. We care about student learning when we diagnosis why they learn or fail to learn. Enjoy the weekend.
Nelson

Enhancing Classroom Instruction No. 116: Working at Different Paces
[Methods] [02/10/20]
Good morning, professors. Please briefly consider the importance of keeping all students engaged during in-class exercises, when students complete their work at different paces.

You may have noticed that certain students, pairs of students, or student groups working on engagement exercises in your classes will finish those exercises well ahead of other students. The peril is that those students may then talk off topic, distracting working students, turning an intensive working session into something like relaxed study hall.

Do not discourage students and pairs or groups of students from working ahead at their own pace. Instead, encourage and reward work drive and initiative. Do so by offering multiple advanced exercises, in the nature of extended studies or extra credit, for those students finishing work ahead of others. Prepare and offer multiple staged exercises, even when your class goal is to complete fewer exercises. Then, when you see the first few students completing the on-task exercise, pause everyone's work just briefly enough to encourage all students to move ahead to another specific exercise when done. Do not rush students who have not yet completed the initial, core exercise. Rather, let each student, pair, or group work at their own pace.

Given that you are a law professor, you were probably one of these advanced students who flew through basic in-class work, ready to gobble up more-advanced exercises. You may even remember teachers who rewarded your skill and discipline with that extra opportunity to advance your learning beyond the class objectives. Be one of those instructors who respects the advanced skill and work drive of higher-achieving students. All students in class will respect you for doing so. Enjoy the week.

Nelson

Enhancing Classroom Instruction No. 117: Sharing and Fading Rubrics

[Assessment] [02/11/20]

Good morning, professors. Please consider this brief note about a technique that may help your students adjust their performance to your standards.

Most of us wisely use a scoring rubric for papers and essay answers on exams. Some of us also share the rubric (minus any exam-specific content) before the exam or paper due date so that students can see in clearest perform, and practice against, the precise standard.

Have you thought, though, of sharing the rubric during the exam, as part of the exam itself? If you give several exams across the term, then sharing the rubric on the first and maybe second or third exam can help students check and confirm their performance. You can then fade the support (eliminate the rubric) on the latter exams by which time students will have incorporated the performance standard.

Below is a vignette recording just such an observation of the value of sharing, and later fading, rubrics. I hope you find something useful here. Enjoy the week.

Nelson

Movement in the classroom's front row caught the professor's attention. The professor was proctoring a fifty-minute interim assessment that ended with an essay question. About forty minutes had passed, and the student who caught the professor's attention appeared to have finished the essay, flipping back and forth as she looked through her answer. The professor looked more closely. The student was checking off points on the rubric that the professor had supplied with the exam, using the rubric to ensure that her essay answer was complete. On the advice of the instructional-design team, the professor had included the rubric with the first couple of interim assessments for exactly that purpose, to help the students self-assess as they performed. The professor would remove the rubric for the last three exams. He graded the student's answer shortly later: a perfect score.

Enhancing Classroom Instruction No. 118: Valuing Subjective Evaluation
[Assessment] [02/12/20]
Good morning, professors. Please consider these brief comments about the value of subjective comments beyond the critical objective scoring rubric.

We all know the necessity of using a model answer and scoring rubric that objectify evaluation of exams. Students should see the standard against which we evaluate their work. Yet subjective comments can add value to the feedback that your objective rubric supplies. Your written can sometimes better explain the objective rubric score. Also, some performances are more general or more subtle, and some criteria less clearly defined, than an objectified rubric can capture.

Students may also do things, whether correct or incorrect, that the rubric did not anticipate, about which they may benefit from your comments. Students may gain insight from your observation of their actions that do not fall within the performance goal. For example, you may teach doctrine, thus not scoring writing quality, but you may wish to communicate that a student's writing obscured an answer, so that the student pay greater attention to writing or seeks writing instruction.

Written comments can also address student motivation. Encouraging comments about small, subordinate parts of an underperforming student's work may countenance and temper an especially low overall score. Likewise, comments further elevating the positive impact of a high score can create greater motivation effect. Consider offering substantial subjective written comments. An example from a Week 4 interim exam, also scored using an objective rubric, appears below. Enjoy the rest of the week.

Nelson

"Reasonably helpful issue statement especially as to law, although you didn't mention what the product was. Be sure to make the fact context reasonably clear. Strong rule section identifying and defining both tests including naming and defining all seven factors of the risk/utility test. You also named the three defect forms and so did a little extra. You chose the stronger test for your analysis, which you began with a helpful preliminary evaluation of the claim, foreshadowing your analysis. That technique can focus your reader's concentration. Your analysis then took each factor in order, letting the factor fall either way rather than trying to justify your position, which is a sound way to analyze. In other words, you balanced the argument nicely. I also respect your judgment. You had a mature, sensible way of treating the factors, seeing both the strength of the claim and its problem. The claim was odd in that way that it was both strong for lack of the flame arrester and weak in that the camper poured gasoline on a fire, a risk easy to avoid and of which the camper should have been aware. You saw that tension between a strong and weak claim, all in one, because you let the factors speak for themselves while you were thoughtful and sound in their application. You have strong analytic skills. Your conclusion was brief when you might have elaborated, but your analysis carried the day. Thank you, and keep at it."

Enhancing Classroom Instruction No. 119: Controlling for Improvement
[Assessment] [02/13/20]

Good morning, professors. Have you had the disappointment of giving students clear feedback but then seeing them consistently fail to implement it? Are you frustrated at students failing to do as your feedback on interim assessments clearly prescribes?

Behavior analysts recognize that prescribing an improvement is not enough. One must often take the additional step of controlling for the consistent incorporation of the improvement. We tend to repeat performances, even when we know that they are weak or wrong. Controls influence and ensure that performance changes when it should.

Look at the second page of the attached scoring rubric for an example of a modest control form. The rubric's second page requires the student to read the first-page feedback, write that feedback in the student's own words on the second page, and commit in writing on the second page to a plan to incorporate that feedback.

Can you think of ways to control for students to incorporate your assessment feedback? We may be doing everything right in giving prompt, clear, objective feedback, yet failing to adequately control for its sound use. Enjoy the rest of the week.
Nelson

Enhancing Classroom Instruction No. 120: Varying Strategic Roles
[Assessment] [02/14/20]
Good morning, professors. Consider this brief note about how we help students both prepare for practice and distinguish critical versus variable attributes, when our problems and exams vary the parties' strategic interests and roles.

Sound test design, the MBE's psychometricians tell us, involves using party roles (landowner, neighbor, manufacturer) rather than proper nouns (Shamika, Miriam, Bert). Proper nouns introduce an associational challenge ("Wait, which one, again, is the plaintiff??!!") that has nothing to do with the exam's knowledge-and-skill-measurement goal. You may have tired, though, of repeatedly using the same roles: prosecutor, police officer, suspect, in criminal cases; landowner, neighbor, tenant, in property cases; and so on.

To construct authentic, relevant, and varied problems and exams, your party roles do not have to be, and in many instances should not be, the legal ones around which you construct your problems. Your fact scenarios should vary widely, as law practice varies widely. The party roles should be scenario-specific roles, not law-specific roles. Your problems may cite public officials, financiers, octogenarians, and the myriad of other roles relevant to your widely varying, authentic scenarios. Using and varying proper nouns (Sekou, Tatania, Duke) doesn't educate students in the many contexts in which law applies. Varying roles widely does.

Be appropriately creative in drafting practice-relevant scenarios that introduce and educate students to their coming rich practice context. Doing so may increase student interest and engagement, while serving an appropriate psychometric goal. See an illustrating teaching scenario below. Enjoy the weekend.
Nelson

The professor chuckled as he scanned down the long lists of hundreds of multiple-choice questions. Their alphabetical order accentuated something that he hadn't until then noticed: they involved dozens if not hundreds of different characters. Sure, several questions, especially the constitutional-law and criminal-procedure questions, involved *public officials, prosecutors,* or *police officers,* but those subjects also had questions about a *junkyard dealer, priest,* and *marijuana retailer.* A few of the real-property questions involved *home buyers* and *sellers,* or *lakefront owners,* but other questions involved *print shops, soda fountains,* and *movie lots.* A few of the tort-law questions involved *manufacturers* and *careless drivers,* but others involved a *hockey player, drone operator,* or *sea captain.* Some of the questions involved a *financier* or *short seller,* while others involved a *press operator* or *cardiologist.* None of the questions, though, involved a *law professor* or *law student.* Too easy and too unreal, the professor thought with another chuckle.

Enhancing Classroom Instruction No. 121: Student Feedback Example
[Methods] [02/17/20]
Good morning, professors. Stevie shares with us, below, some student feedback she received on one of her in-class exercises, confirming the value of her design. Soliciting feedback can not only confirm or correct designs but also shows students how much you care about their learning. Kudos to Stevie. See her introduction and the student comments below. And enjoy the week.
Nelson

"I had students work in teams on highlighting 'bullet point' responses from a short essay distributed in my Property II class last week. When we went over it, I called on various teams to discuss their responses to the three part answer. I asked if any students wanted to share feedback from the experience. Here are the two responses that I received:

"'I liked the group work activity from last class, and I found the collaboration to be beneficial. Issue spotting in a group is a useful activity for working out how everyone runs through the issue spotting process';

"'The group essay exercise we completed in Property II class this morning was quite helpful! It was nice to talk out loud with other students and to see where everyone's understanding was with the material that we have covered so far in these past three weeks. Big takeaway, especially with shorter/simpler essays is that even though sometimes things may be obvious and simple, it's important to remember to write it out on the essays to ensure proper points are awarded.'"

Enhancing Classroom Instruction No. 122: Survey for Student Feedback
[Assessment] [02/18/20]
Good morning, professors. This link is to a Google form (survey) that you may copy into your own Google drive and then modify and use to solicit student feedback.

I designed and used this form to ask for student feedback on course methods and course resources, but you may ask students about anything you wish relevant to instruction: course methods and resources, yes, but also assessment form, assessment schedule, assessment feedback, teaching assistants, lecture style, slideshow quality, casebook value, you name it.

Please don't share this specific form with your students but instead first use the "Make a Copy" command so that you are sharing your own survey. Once you make a copy, you can rename the form as you choose and move it wherever you wish. A survey or two each term to each class gets you timely feedback while communicating to students that you are investing your creative skills in their instruction. Enjoy the rest of the week.
Nelson

Enhancing Classroom Instruction No. 123: Preferred Feedback Qualities
[Assessment] [02/19/20]
Good morning, professors. Please consider these suggestions about the quality of the feedback comments that you share with students, whether in writing relating to a paper or assessment, or in person in office or in class. The quality of your feedback influences whether students can and will make use of it or not.

First, make your feedback descriptive more so than evaluative. Telling students that they *did this and did not do that* helps students accept your critique and adjust accordingly, while telling students that their *work was weak* leaves them without a guide and spurs defensiveness.

Also, make feedback specific to the student's responses, as in *your issue statement didn't include the parties' strategic roles*, more so than general, as in *your answer was vague*. Specific feedback enables correction, while general feedback can frustrate a student who is unable to identify the work warranting the critique.

In general, give feedback on things students can correct and control for correction. Provide feedback when students can act on it, not after it's too late. Connect your feedback to instruction and its goals. And make your feedback clear. Ambiguous feedback that the student misinterprets can do more harm than good.

Finally, consider soliciting students for the kind of feedback that they would like to have. They may surprise you how willing they are to have you evaluate their work critically. Whether accepted or not, your invitation reveals your interest in their improvement, which may spur them to greater effort. I hope these tips help. Enjoy the rest of the week.
Nelson

Enhancing Classroom Instruction No. 124: More Options than You Think
[Methods] [02/20/20]
Good morning, professors. Teaching at times can seem like a relatively rigid routine, but you may have more options than you think, for small changes that make big differences, especially in the all-important frequency building. You may be able to change:

- when the exercise occurs, moving engagement from earlier to later in the class, or later to earlier, or to another week;
- where the exercise occurs, moving from a tiered, fixed-seating, forward-looking-seating classroom to a flat classroom with round tables, or from classroom to practice courtroom;
- how often the exercise occurs, such as doubling its frequency if effective or, if stale or of limited effectiveness, halving its frequency;
- consequences of instruction, increasing or decreasing point-value, credit, or other reward;
- presenting stimuli like readings, videos, lectures, and slideshows, eliminating some for others or shortening, clarifying, and summarizing them; and
- the focus (pinpoint) frequency activity (that activity from which other activities build), substituting one activity to another in the cluster of related activities.

These changes can increase attention, effort, urgency, engagement, interest, and accountability, while reducing distraction, depletion, exhaustion, and inattention. Do not underestimate your options and their power and sensitivity to affect learning. Below is an illustrating scenario. Enjoy the last of the week.
Nelson

The reason that the professor liked teaching so much was that every class was a new adventure. Oh, sure, students knew basically what to expect. Her course and each of its classes had a clear structure, with resources aligned to instruction aligned to assessment aligned to objectives. Her instruction was well designed, orderly, and thoughtful, each class having an introduction, relevance demonstration, modeling, discussion stimulus, frequency practice, and feedback. Yet she found that she was constantly varying things in the classroom, not only from course to course and term to term but also from class to class within the term. The variations were mostly subtle. She adopted them sometimes as they came to her from external sources like news, events, conversation, and research. Other times, she simply discerned that students needed a small change, or *she* needed a small change, for the sake of changing. Above all, she wanted students to appreciate that the subject itself was inexhaustible--even though ancient, nevertheless still a constant flow of creativity and new energy.

Enhancing Classroom Instruction No. 125: Contingency Management
[Research] [02/21/20]
Good morning, professors. Please consider this abstract of the attached article on *Contingency Management* by behavior analyst B.F. Skinner.

Students learn whether we teach them or not. The important questions are how much, how fast, and what they learn. In that sense, to teach simply means to direct and hasten learning toward the desired goal. This precise and natural definition highlights that teaching must involve *managing the contingencies that influence behavior*. We can do whatever we wish in the classroom, but if what we do is not influencing student behavior toward the desired learning goal, then we aren't teaching.

We hope that students are acting on their classroom (and other) learning environment to produce consequences including knowledge, skill, good grades, graduation, bar passage, and employment. Effective instruction focuses its contingencies on students' operant behavior--again, where they act on their environment to produce learning. Effective instruction also prefers positive reinforcement, such as the natural encouragement of knowing promptly that they have behaved appropriately (recalled accurate law, applied law analytically, articulated right answers).

Traditional education employs too many aversive controls (low marks, chastisement, fear), hiding the proverbial ball to ensure that achieving learning goals is more difficult than it need be so that aversive controls retain their power. Traditional education further avoids behavioral objectives that one can see students achieve, in favor of unobservable objectives that one cannot see and measure, thus retaining and amplifying the instructor's power over students.

Fascinatingly, effective reinforcement works better when its contingencies remain undefined. If students know in advance how to obtain a reward, then they alter their behavior to reward-seeking over the broader and deeper learning goal. Effective instruction thus must employ contingencies without always making them apparent. The learning goal should be apparent, and the instruction clear, but the contingency triggering the reinforcement should remain hidden and varying to keep students focused on the learning goal over reward-seeking.

Learn and value the deep principles on which we can base enhanced instruction. Explore the wisdom of those who expose the faults in traditional instruction while discerning a better course. And enjoy the weekend.

Nelson

Enhancing Classroom Instruction No. 126: Teaching Thinking Like a Lawyer

[Methods] [02/24/20]

Good morning, professors. Please consider this brief insight on the challenge of teaching students to think like lawyers.

Law schools commonly conceive of their goal as teaching students to think like lawyers. That conception immediately handicaps professors in that one cannot observe thinking. Professors have no direct means of determining whether the contingencies that their instruction arranges produce that which they take as their goal. Professors must instead infer student thinking from what students do. Thinking's observable behaviors are generally what students say or write, and sometimes what they choose.

That teaching must necessarily produce observable speaking, writing, and choosing, addresses a common failing of law instruction, which is that it primarily entails the professor rather than the student speaking, writing, and choosing. Professors should instead arrange instruction's contingencies to produce abundant student speaking, writing, and choosing. Instruction should spur frequent student production of overt performance goals, with prompt feedback and positive consequences.

Try deemphasizing the covert thinking goal, while emphasizing the overt speaking, writing, and choosing performances. Evaluate and adjust your instruction accordingly, and the results may surprise you. Enjoy the week.

Nelson

Enhancing Classroom Instruction No. 127: Concept Formation

[Methods] [02/25/20]

Good morning, professors. Please consider this brief note about analyzing concepts closely to design efficient instruction in concept formation.

You may sense tension between wanting to see students speak, write, and choose as they must to accomplish instruction's goals, while at the same time fostering the sound concept formation on which students must base correct performance. Law professors tend to overemphasize concept formation to the detriment of performance practice, which may be natural given law's highly cognitive nature. How does a skilled instructor support covert concept formation while ensuring correct performance?

Direct instruction analyzes instructional sequences forming complex knowledge, especially the fine discriminations that students must make to acquire a sound knowledge base. Professors skilled at direct instruction offer abundant practice with prompt feedback correcting errors and reinforcement for correct performance. Yet they also analyze the knowledge forms, chunking them into appropriate sequences for students to master through discrimination training before assembling them into the complex final knowledge.

Attend closely to concept formation, analyzing knowledge systems to draw out for students their similarity and distinctions. Do so, though, while offering sequenced practice in the components of those knowledge systems. Both analysis and practice are important. Enjoy the week.
Nelson

Enhancing Classroom Instruction No. 128: Near Non-Examples
[Methods] [02/26/20]
Good morning, professors. Please consider this brief note about the significant role of near non-examples in rigorous concept formation, drawn from studies of direct instruction. To know a concept requires the ability not just to recognize examples but also to distinguish the examples from near non-examples. Positive examples do not sufficiently form a concept. Instruction must also display negative examples, if students are to learn the concept's distinct attributes, limits, and contours.

Studies show that for negative examples to rule out the greatest number of possible concept misinterpretations, they should be as close to the concept as possible, without falling within the concept—a near non-example. Studies also show that students learn most quickly from continuous conversion of the positive example to the negative example, rather than from discontinuous presentation of separate positive and negative examples. Make your non-examples extensions of your examples. If you cannot make a continuous presentation from example to non-example, then studies show that keeping the presentation setup (context) the same for the positive and negative examples aids concept formation.

Also, presenting one positive example or even a narrow range of positive examples does not sufficiently form the concept. Studies show that instruction must display a wide range of examples for students to distinguish the concept's critical criteria from non-critical variables associated with common presentations of the concept. Avoid presenting examples that have irrelevant commonalities. Studies show that students will incorrectly assume that irrelevant commonalities are critical attributes of the concept. Appreciate the value of these direct-instruction principles. Consider using example / near-non-example worksheets to help students with rigorous concept formation. Enjoy the rest of the week.
Nelson

Enhancing Classroom Instruction No. 129: Lengthy Readings
[Methods] [02/27/20]
Good morning, professors. Please consider this brief note about reading and its skill. Many of us assign lengthy readings from poorly drafted casebooks, unfortunately limiting students' ability to use effective reading-study techniques. That students vary from expert to novice in their reading and comprehension skills accentuates the reading challenge.

First, consider carefully the length and quality of the readings that you assign. Then, help students draw the most from their reading by introducing techniques like the SQ3R method to *survey, question, read, recite, and review*. Offer end-of-class surveys of upcoming readings. Supply questions and problems for student review in advance of reading. Students will then read with greater focus and engagement.

Rereading, though popular, supplies limited benefit, especially when students have insufficient time to reread lengthy assignments. Taking notes while reading, another popular technique, supplies much greater benefit due to the more-active processing and its encoding effect, yet less benefit when simply noting material without restating, rearranging, and analyzing.

Reciting from the text (free recall) supplies longer-term benefit, as does review of the text for organization, but the benefit dissipates for subjects requiring application and inference. A better practice is for students to read and recite to *make judgments and inferences from their recall.* Embedding questions in the text or in online videos promotes judgment and inference, strengthening long-term recall. Online presentations that require students to complete questions before continuing enhances study value.

Help your students read productively. Disparate reading skills may account for much of the disparity in student performance. Wise practices on your part can level the reading playing field. Enjoy the rest of the week and weekend.
Nelson

Enhancing Classroom Instruction No. 130: Reading Myths
[Research] [02/28/20]
Good morning, professors. Please consider this brief research summary dispelling some reading myths, drawn from Arthur Whimbey's classic text *Problem Solving and Comprehension.* You may be able to help students correct some of these myths.

First, convention discourages students from subvocalizing (moving lips, whispering to oneself) when reading. Yet close studies show that subvocalizing is at least helpful and perhaps critical for reading complex material, significantly improving comprehension. Reading complex material is like solving a mathematics problem, requiring great attention to definition, detail, and relationships within the information. Encourage students to speak to themselves and one another, formulating words and thoughts interpreting the text as they read--to read aloud, paraphrase, question, interpret, and confirm understanding as they read. Demonstrate those techniques when you read text in class.

Second, convention encourages students to focus on key words such as nouns, adjectives, adverbs, and active verbs, when to the contrary reading all text (every word) can be critical to comprehending complex

material. Readers have no ready procedure for identifying key words. Articles, prepositions, conjunctions, and other ordinary-looking words are often critical. While convention suggests that speed reading is possible and desirable, comprehension requires slower reading, even reading word by word. Sound reading requires attention, care, caution, diligence, and thoroughness. Help students recognize that myths tend to propagate shortcuts that don't work. Enjoy the weekend.
Nelson

Enhancing Classroom Instruction No. 131: Remarkable Insights
[Research] [03/02/20]
Good morning, professors. Please consider some special instructional insights that behavior analysts Thomas and Marilyn Gilbert developed from rigorous analysis of instruction, summarized in their classic journal article at this link.

One principle their studies proved is to *group together concepts that students easily confuse* so that students can see and learn their distinctions. You might, for instance, deliberately teach strict liability (for abnormally dangerous activities) right after strict products liability, and contrast on a single slide their distinct Second Restatement tests, to highlight their differences. My doing so eliminated student confusion between the subjects and their tests.

Another principle that their studies discovered is to *teach the hard things first*. They proved, for instance, that you can teach children their multiplication tables in an hour, in a way that they'll never forget. One must, though, start with the difficult sixes, sevens, and eights. Otherwise, the instruction from twos and threes toward the hardest sevens and eights is progressively more difficult, discouraging rather than encouraging students (in effect punishing rather than rewarding them for advancing).

Through precise testing, the Gilberts discovered forty total principles, including the above two, that operate in the opposite fashion than traditional instruction presumes. The Gilberts' short article calmly lampoons ineffective instructional techniques, both those of traditional instruction and their own when poorly designed. Read the article not only for its special insights but for their scientific approach and precise vocabulary of learning. Enjoy the week.
Nelson

Enhancing Classroom Instruction No. 132: Encoding Reading
[Research] [03/03/20]
Good morning, professors. Please consider this brief insight on the role of reading in learning, drawn in part from Skinner's classic *The Technology of Teaching*.

Reading's objective is not memorized words. Instead, the objective is that the student build knowledge structures to retain long enough to pursue the performance goal toward which the professor assigned the reading. Yet to a degree, skilled readers do initially memorize what they read, just long enough to create and preserve more-lasting knowledge structures.

Memory aids like pause-and-rehearse techniques aid transitional memorizing. Employing alliteration, or constructing lyrical phrases, can also help. More-elaborate aids, like taking the first letter of each of several consecutive words to form a memorable construct, can help further. Skilled readers may also form partial, loose, shifting mnemonics as a subtly exercised transfer strategy. Encourage students to practice these techniques overtly to build covert use, as skilled readers typically exercise them. And enjoy the week.
Nelson

Enhancing Classroom Instruction No. 133: IRAC as Algorithm
[Methods] [03/04/20]
Good morning, professors. Please consider this note about how we can aid learning by showing how lawyers follow algorithms or heuristics to practice law reliably and efficiently. In performing tasks, lawyers and other professionals follow sequences from one simple task to another, to build the complex services and products that they offer. Students learn those complex services by practicing their simpler components.

Algorithms, or in other parlance *heuristics*, are shorter pieces of those long chain-like sequences, connecting or clustering few-enough steps to make the work manageable. Yet algorithms are often covert, relying on cognitive rather than psychomotor responses. Help students see the algorithms or heuristics. Have them explain their thoughts so that you can correct their process errors. Demonstrate problem solutions step by step, articulating explicitly each algorithm step.

The IRAC construct is an example heuristic within which lawyers embed other heuristics. We all know IRAC. But help students see that sound statements of the issue themselves involve three components (law, fact context, and party tension). Help them see that sound rule statements involve framework, core rule, definition, and limits or exceptions. Help them see the heuristic for strong analysis and for a value-add conclusion. Embed heuristics within heuristics until students perform comprehensively, accurately, and reliably, and efficiently. And enjoy the rest of the week.
Nelson

Enhancing Classroom Instruction No. 134: Learning Rules
[Research] [03/05/20]
Good morning, professors. Consider this brief note about what learning a rule means and how it occurs. Learning rules involves generalizing them to situations to which they apply. Generalizing a rule to apply to other situations than the example given on the rule's first presentation requires that students identify the new situation as the same in relevant attributes as the initial rule illustration.

Put another way, students must gradually recognize which examples fall within the rule and what are the common attributes those examples share. Every successive application of the rule in a new situation to which it applies increases the reliability of the generalization, until the student has a full sense of the rule's contours, meaning that the student can identify shared attributes of different situations.

So how do students generalize rules? Studies suggest that students follow three operations to generalize rules: interpolation; extrapolation; and stipulation. Interpolation includes within the rule a different dimension of the same attribute. Extrapolation excludes from the rule a greater dimension than a dimension already ruled out. Stipulation specifies as within the rule single examples of similar dimension.

Socratic examination often explores interpolation, extrapolation, and stipulation, although it does so one student at a time under stressful circumstances without directly engaging other students. Well-designed exercises can supply more students with greater practice. Note how your instruction helps students generalize rules. And enjoy the rest of the week.

Nelson

Enhancing Classroom Instruction No. 135: Teaching Through Examples
[Research] [03/06/20]

Good morning, professors. Please consider these brief tips drawn from Professors Siegfried Engelmann and Douglas Carnine's masterful *Theory of Instruction,* on how to teach through examples.

First, present initial examples only briefly so that students do not unduly limit the new concept's attributes to one example.

Next, use multiple examples. One example does not teach a concept.

Next, use negative (non-) examples. Examples that are all positive examples leave open other interpretations.

Next, when using positive and negative examples, make common as many of their attributes as possible, to rule out possible misinterpretation.

Next, make negative examples close to positive examples. Negative examples rule out the most misinterpretations when they are least different from positive examples. You also reduce the number of positive and negative examples necessary to illustrate distinctions, when contrasting examples and non-examples are most alike.

Then, make positive examples as unlike one another as possible, thereby more-clearly isolating the common features.

Then, when sequencing examples, use similar wording to make the sequence obvious. But when testing example and non-example recognition, select examples and non-examples that have no predictable relationship. Do not design the test setup to trigger the response. Instead, let students discern the correct response from their generalization and discrimination.

I hope you find something useful in these insightful tips. Enjoy the weekend.

Nelson

Enhancing Classroom Instruction No. 136: Dr. Johnson Paper on Instruction

[Research] [03/09/20]

Good morning, professors. WMU grad student Kyle Kenny shares with us, at this link, a paper outlining some helpful history of behavior-based instructional design. Although the whole paper holds interest, consider reading starting at the middle of page seventeen for the four categories of learning relationships.

You'll see in the articulation of those categories much of the challenge that we face in helping students master complex knowledge, starting with proper responses, then at the proper time, then under novel circumstances, and finally with appropriate emotional relations.

You may also see why you are helping students do certain things, how those things may relate to other things you are helping students do, and how you might alter some performance conditions, contingencies, or rewards to speed and refine learning.

If you do find the time, then make a quick review of the first third of the paper for a history of the development of teaching machines, programmed instruction, and computer-based instruction, toward which higher education continues to creep. Knowing the time and paradigm within which we work may help us not only teach better but also sleep better. Enjoy the week.

Nelson

Enhancing Classroom Instruction No. 137: Feedback Study

[Research] [03/10/20]

Good morning, professors. Please consider this brief abstract of a study on the effect of different kinds of exam feedback, or review the study's summary itself at this link, to confirm some obvious things that you likely already know.

In this study, the authors conclude that students simply learning about exam results, like receiving a certain grade or score, has the least data to support that feedback's efficacy. No surprise: results alone don't matter much to improving performance.

The authors do find efficacy to exam feedback that tells students whether their response was correct or incorrect. Again, no surprise: learning that one is performing correctly or incorrectly on specific test items helps to improve next performance at least some.

Here, though, is the most-powerful finding: elaboration feedback, which is feedback explaining why performance was correct or incorrect, correlates most strongly with improved exam performance. Again, no surprise: developing the means (the rubrics) and taking the time to provide evaluation reasoning has the greatest effect on improving performance.

Sometimes, studies confirm the obvious. And sometimes, improving our own performance just takes doing the obvious. Enjoy the week.
Nelson

Enhancing Classroom Instruction No. 138: Studies on the Testing Effect
[Research] [03/11/20]
Good morning, professors. Please consider this brief abstract of the article at this link, supplied by the WMU grad-student team, summarizing many studies showing the benefit of the testing effect. The article concludes that testing and self-testing remain underutilized as educational approaches, for all their learning benefits.

Testing is effective because while lectures, outline review, and similar passive activities promote recognition, testing can instead promote recall, not only on the test but also in preparing for the test. Recall is more powerful in building lasting memories and in organizing concepts into use structures.

The most-effective tests are those that prioritize recall over recognition, require application of the recalled concepts, repeat topic review at spaced intervals over time, provide explanatory feedback, and encourage students to self-test in preparation, supplying quality aligned practice.

Standardized pre-graduation tests, though, are no substitute for improved curricula and instruction.

WMU grad-student Kyle Kenny supplied this article in answer to a question that I posed to him about whether to test cumulatively every three weeks or only over each three weeks of material. Appreciate how empirical studies can answer basic questions like this one: cumulative testing has the better effect. Enjoy the rest of the week.
Nelson

Enhancing Classroom Instruction No. 139: Example Ranges
[Methods] [03/12/20]
Good morning, professors. Please consider this brief note suggesting how to refine a common practice in which you surely routinely engage: choosing examples to illustrate new concepts.

The challenge of learning law can be that the doctrines apply in so many different circumstances. Learning law requires that students generalize and discriminate where concepts apply, which means careful choice of examples and non-examples. As instructors, we are constantly giving examples. The examples we choose influence learning.

For simple concepts, choose examples anywhere within the concept's boundaries, to speed learning. For difficult concepts, though, keep early examples that close to the concept's core, to highlight common settings and critical attributes. Choosing examples at the boundaries instead of the core may cause students to misidentify critical attributes. Successive illustrations may then step farther from the core and closer to the concept's boundaries.

Similarly, choose highly distinct non-examples to introduce a difficult concept, to ensure that students do not confuse variable attributes for critical attributes. Then, choose successive non-examples that approach the concept's boundaries, so that students can refine and confirm their concept discrimination. We all choose many examples. A little extra thought in their selection can speed learning. Enjoy the last of the week.
Nelson

Enhancing Classroom Instruction No. 140: Motivation
[Research] [03/13/20]
Good morning, professors. Please consider this brief note about motivation, drawn from the chapter *Motivation Theory in Educational Practice* authored by professors Kaplan, Katz, and Flum.

Definitions of motivation differ, whether narrowly as to concrete actions that students take in specific situations or broadly across situations. Psychologists also differ on the locus of motivation, whether in the student or in stimuli, or a mix of the two. Motivation may just be a way of describing a student's results. Whatever motivation is, if anything more than illusory, it obviously varies widely among students.

The question that instructors ask is, can we affect it? Psychologists differ on how stable motivation is. If motivation is a deep-seated, stable trait, then instruction may have little effect in shaping it. If, on the other hand, motivation is malleable, then instruction may have effect. Motivation literature suggests the following educational practices to influence motivation, assuming meaning to that illusory construct:

• employ meaningful and relevant study activities;
• promote challenging, achievable, proximate objectives;
• adjust challenges to student confidence, attitude, and skill level;
• promote perception of student control;
• encourage student focus on mastering outcomes;
• supply variety, novelty, imagination, and humor; and
• provide accurate feedback focused on diagnosis and prescription.

I hope you find something helpful in this brief review of a chapter summarizing the literature of motivation. Enjoy the weekend.
Nelson

Enhancing Classroom Instruction No. 141: Superordinate and Subordinate
[Methods] [03/16/20]
Good morning, professors. Please consider this brief note about helping students recognize different relationships of linked concepts.

Obvious to us is that one of two or more related concepts is either superordinate to the other concept, subordinate to the other concept, or coordinate with the other concept. For example, a claim is superordinate to its elements, an element subordinate to its claim, and elements coordinate to one another. For another example, alternative definitions of an element are subordinate to the element that they define, while coordinate to one another and superordinate to a condition, factor, or criterion that is a part of the definition.

Again, these relationships are obvious to us. Yet in the jumble of new concepts that students encounter week to week in any one course, their relationships will not always be so obvious to students. Thus, our presentations should make those relationships especially clear. We should then design practice to help students recognize, recall, and apply the different relationships of concept to concept. Give students presentations and practice in the content structure, as much as in the content itself. The structure helps solidify the content. And enjoy the week.
Nelson

Enhancing Classroom Instruction No. 142: WMU Instructional-Design Team
[Resources] [03/17/20]
Good morning, professors. Please consider this brief note about the skills that the WMU Instructional-Design Research Lab grad students bring to us as a study and innovation resource. Lawyers consult experts all the time. Law professors can, too.

One grad student working with two law professors this term has already served as a process-design and performance-management consultant for a major craft brewer. After extensive investigation, his design team discerned specific inefficiencies in certain processes, that the team was then able to address and correct with refined procedures, task clarification, measurable goals, and performance feedback.

Another grad student working with other law professors this term has worked as an organizational-development specialist investigating WMU's facility management for opportunities to design initiatives to improve operational performance in business processes and management practices. The student developed and standardized operating procedures for several functions and processes, including professional work, creating job aids and checklists.

What does this design resource mean to us? One law professor who for the first time accepted a WMU grad student as an in-class observer this term has given the grad student's work rave reviews, especially the sensitivity that the grad student has shown in affirming the professor's already-outstanding instructional-design work. The grad students, whom Dr. Johnson selects competitively for this program, are not only astute observers but also sound of character and wise beyond their years. Consider consulting with them for their expertise. And enjoy the week.
Nelson

Enhancing Classroom Instruction No. 143: Stimulus Equivalence's Power
[Research] [03/18/20]
Good morning, professors. Please consider this brief abstract of the attached article on a mysteriously powerful teaching method that increases implicit learning without adding explicit instruction. You may already use this method without knowing that you do and without knowing how well it works for you.

Stimulus equivalence, or *equivalence-based instruction,* involves teaching how one concept relates to two other concepts, allowing the learner to associate those two other concepts with one another, without any such direct instruction. Imagine that: to learn generatively, intuitively, without the time necessary for presenting stimuli and shaping responses. This generative learning educators call *transitivity* or *transitive inference.*

The study the attached article describes confirmed that equivalence-based instruction can work in college courses, not just for basic learning where the method already has significant acceptance. Remember, the idea is to teach the relationship of one concept to a second, and then that same first concept to a third concept, so that students naturally associate the second and third concepts. I hope you can see how you might already be using this method. Enjoy the last of the week.
Nelson

Enhancing Classroom Instruction No. 144: Fluency as Core Goal
[Research] [03/19/20]

Good morning, professors. Please consider this brief abstract of the attached article, summarizing the development of the concept of fluency. Recall that our WMU collaborator Dr. Johnson's initial insight was that to increase bar passage, instruction should increase fluency. See if to you this fluency phenomenon doesn't sound like it relates closely to bar-exam conditions.

Fluency implies both the speed and accuracy of performance. The frequency with which your instruction produces and sustains student behavior relates strongly to student retention, performance maintenance, endurance, resistance to distraction, concept application, and performance transfer. Fluency-based instruction, focusing on fluency aims, can significantly improve education and training, while producing unprecedented efficiency gains.

Fluency training, within the field of precision teaching, involves introducing relatively brief periods of timed, intensive performance, measured for speed and accuracy, and monitored for meeting acceptable rates of performance. Accuracy alone is not enough. One must also perform speedily and consistently enough, to meet minimum performance conditions. The field called these retention-endurance-application performance standards.

Fascinatingly, increasing performance frequencies also increases skill in application. Frequency building, helping students use simpler concepts with greater ease, speed, and consistency, increases their ability to use those concepts for the more-complex work of application, to an extent *even without instruction in that application.* Yes, start with concept acquisition. But then, don't skip the step of frequency building before proceeding to application and adaptation.

These are just a few of the attached article's insights. Keep fluency building in mind. And enjoy the last of the week.
Nelson

Enhancing Classroom Instruction No. 145: Fading Prompts
[Methods] [03/20/20]
Good morning, professors. Please consider this brief note about *fading prompts* that may alert you to a technique that you already use, while better informing you about its role in your instruction.

116

Instructors properly prompt students to perform. A question call, for instance, is a prompt, as is an oral question during Socratic examination and, when the student stumbles, a hint toward the expected performance. Indeed, prompts, such as question calls, can be specific or broad, depending on the student's ability to discern correct performance without the prompt. You very likely already vary your question calls from specific to broad, depending on student ability to spot and address critical issues.

Lawyers practice with few, if any, prompts, but students plainly need prompts when mastering subject performance. Prompts thus play a critical role in instruction, but *so does their fading*. If instruction continues to provide prompts beyond their need, rather than fading them, then instruction inhibits rather than aids learning. Prompts are appropriate only to induce students to initiate a performance that they cannot otherwise begin.

Do not prompt when students requires no prompt. Prompting continuously without soon desisting discourages students from building the frequency necessary to perform without the prompt. Don't encourage students to rely on prompts. Instead, withdraw prompts as soon as you are able. If you must prompt repeatedly to induce performance, then gradually introduce interfering stimuli between the prompt and response so that students rely less on prompts and begin to perform with the prompt receding.

Be aware of the technique and role of prompts, but also be aware of fading or vanishing prompts. If the goal requires performing without prompts, then use them judiciously and sensitively so as not to inhibit student acquisition of requisite skill and knowledge. And enjoy the weekend.
Nelson

Enhancing Classroom Instruction No. 146: Group Versus Individual Work
[Methods] [03/23/20]
Good morning, professors. Please consider this brief note about how to support individual academic progress, as the bar exam makes absolutely necessary, in the context of group studies.

Group work develops teamwork, communication, and leadership skills, while recruiting engagement and facilitating student-to-student instruction, all of enormous potential value. Yet graduates must each pass the bar exam individually and may practice law so as well. Every student must therefore meet performance goals, no matter how well group work may serve some. Behavioral designs that analyze, chunk, and sequence instruction into staged and guided exercises facilitate both group and individual learning. These designs tend to meet each student at the level they require, permitting them to proceed at their own pace.

Watch your pairs work in class. Some pairs race ahead, while others go quite slow. Listen closely, and you should notice that the slow pairs are helping one another discern the rules and correct and improve performance. Don't rush them. They may be working exactly where they need to work. Yet also don't hold the fast pairs back, when they are meeting the performance goals. When you chunk and sequence learning, students enter at their own level and proceed at their own pace across multiple competencies, whether understanding, recall, application, or evaluation and problem solving. You personalize learning, allowing for variations not only in student level but in preferred pace, place, relationship, formats, and technologies.

Behavioral designs feel more personal because they are more personal. Keep creating multiple entry and exit points for students, grouping studies so that students can proceed quickly or slowly, knowing that they are meeting performance goals. And enjoy the week.
Nelson

Enhancing Classroom Instruction No. 147: Attributes Analysis
[Methods] [03/24/20]
Good morning, professors. Please consider this brief note about the value of having students make an attributes analysis of one or more of your subject's complex rules. The WMU instructional-design team shared this concept with us some time ago.

Law is proscriptive. Lawyers read codes and cases for their clients must do and not do. A single complex case holding, statute, or rule may embed not just one but several proscriptions. Enumerating the proscriptions, as in "do this and don't do that," is in part how lawyers understand, apply, and communicate law. Yet proscriptions can be easy to miss, until one develops the analysis skill. An attributes-analysis exercise helps students develop their skill of recognizing proscriptions and the context in which each proscription applies.

Here's one way to create such an exercise. First, reproduce the complex case holding, statute, rule, restatement, or other law. Count the number of its proscriptions, and then supply that number of blank lines below the law statement, instructing that students identify and write the proscriptions. Supply the first proscription or two to get students started.

On the same exercise sheet, supply several brief one-or-two sentence fact patterns in which your experience teaches you that each proscription would apply. Instruct students to match each proscription to each fact pattern. Finally, request that students generate and write a brief fact pattern for the remaining proscriptions for which they did not find a matching fact pattern.

You will then have helped students both analyze the rule and discern how and when it applies. This exercise takes time, so do it only once in a while, to help students develop the skill, not to teach all or many rules. Enjoy the week.
Nelson

Enhancing Classroom Instruction No. 148: Variable Attributes
[Methods] [03/25/20]
Good morning, professors. Please consider this brief note about the role of variable attributes in rule recognition and how to instruct in that role. Yesterday's message dealt with the proscriptive nature of legal rules and how students must learn and apply each rule's do's and don'ts. In addition to those critical attributes, rules also have variable attributes permitting an action or condition without requiring it. Students need to learn to recognize variable attributes of rules, just as they need to learn critical attributes.

For instance, states recognizing the outrage tort require claimants to prove their severe distress. In any one case, severe distress may or may not lead to work disability or medical expense, although those consequences may frequently follow. Those consequences are thus variable attributes contributing proof to the tort's critical attribute of severe distress. For students to know and apply a rule, they must not only identify critical attributes but also variable attributes. Students who confuse a variable attribute for a critical attribute have not learned the rule.

To instruct in the difference between critical and variable attributes, you must vary the variables. Elements and conditions (critical attributes) gain their definition from contrast with variables that may accompany them. If work disability and medical expense need not exist for distress to be severe, then instruction should show severe distress with and without those variable attributes. Follow a similar exercise for variable attributes that you do for critical attributes, requiring students to recognize variables and illustrate them. And enjoy the rest of the week.
Nelson

Enhancing Classroom Instruction No. 149: Rule Contexts
[Methods] [03/26/20]
Good morning, professors. Please consider this brief note on the role of rule contexts in learning rules.

A rule states a relationship between concepts, guiding actions in certain contexts. For a student to learn a rule means not only that the student recalls it but also applies it in the right context. A key to learning rules is thus to recognize not only the rule's proscriptions but also its applicable context.

Rules often leave unstated or implicit the context in which they apply. Some rules state the context using the introductory word *when*, like, "When filing a complaint, prepare a summons for the court to issue." Yet other rules omit the context, as in, "A summons must accompany the complaint," leaving students to infer from limited knowledge.

Help students recognize, enumerate, and distinguish contexts. Vary contexts thoughtfully in your instruction, so that students can see and learn rule contexts. And enjoy the rest of the week.
Nelson

Enhancing Classroom Instruction No. 150: Problem-Solving Strategies
[Methods] [03/27/20]
Good morning, professors. Please consider communicating to students these brief problem-solving strategies:

1. Maintain a positive attitude that solution is possible, even while recognizing that a problem's first presentation is likely to both confuse and overwhelm;
2. Break down the problem into discrete, manageable, and understandable parts before reassembling the parts into the whole;
3. Demand accuracy, for instance by looking up unknown terms, confirming facts, and cross-checking information for coherency;
4. Address and solve problem parts in sensible order, first steps before second steps;
5. Engage actively. Problems may require new or unconventional solutions that only more-energetic exploration will discover;
6. When stuck, shift perspectives, trying new approaches that facilitate discovery.

Model these strategies for students while helping them apply the strategies in their own work. You, too, be a strategic problem solver, showing students how to do so. And enjoy the weekend.
Nelson

Enhancing Classroom Instruction No. 151: Affect Goals
[Methods] [03/30/20]
Good morning, professors. Please consider this brief vignette on the influence of student affect on achieving academic and law-practice goals:

After years of teaching, the professor finally realized that she had not just academic goals but also an affect goal for every class: that students would make the topic appear flammable, combustible, consuming to themselves. Of course, she wanted students learning doctrine to apply to relevant scenarios. She knew that students needed to pass the bar exam and be able to provide value to clients in law practice. Yet she had finally recognized that they first had to meet the affect goal to achieve those other goals. Students somehow needed to first create or recruit the energy and passion to pour themselves into law studies and, after passing the bar exam, client issues and opportunities. Little is achievable without the affect. And so at every opportunity, she modeled, coached, and mentored the affect, helping students turn their own blow torches on every seemingly intractable problem.

Enjoy exercising your passionate, consuming affect this week, borrowed from the greater depths of your subject.
Nelson

Enhancing Classroom Instruction No. 152: Drafting in Doctrinal Courses
[Methods] [03/31/20]
Good morning, professors. Please consider this brief note suggesting how to introduce students to drafting tasks, even in early (first-term) doctrinal courses.

Sequenced exercises of a behavioral-design class enable you to allow students, student pairs, and groups of students to proceed at different rates. In your engagement-exercise time, you've seen how students who already possess relevant knowledge and skills move more quickly through the exercises.

To introduce students to drafting tasks, end every series of exercises (every class) with a drafting exercise. Advanced students may reach and attempt those exercises. Even if no group, pair, or student do reach the drafting exercise, you can still wind up the engagement period by introducing the drafting task.

Ending each engagement period with a drafting task based on the class's topic is a powerful way of demonstrating the topic's practice context and relevance. Students must believe the knowledge to be valuable, to put forth the effort to learn it. Showing how lawyers use the knowledge in drafting proves value.

If you also sequence drafting exercises across the term, then you can introduce students to all or most foundational tasks within your subject's practice field. No lawyer will ever be able to challenge your students that they "haven't even seen" the relevant practice document before--because they have, in your course.

122

I hope you find something of value here. Please don't hesitate to ask for example drafting exercises. And enjoy the week.
Nelson

Enhancing Classroom Instruction No. 153: Student Misconceptions of Learning
[Research] [04/01/20]
Good morning, professors. Please accept this brief reminder not to underestimate the power and persistence of student misconceptions about learning. Studies summarized in Taylor and Kowalski's book chapter *Student Misconceptions* indicate that false myths about learning persist through higher education in surprisingly high percentages of students, even when instruction contradicts misinformation.

You have likely encountered these examples of wrong attitudes and false myths about learning. Many students believe learning to be fast and easy rather than slow and arduous. Many believe that they need not give full effort. Many believe that learning need not challenge them. Many believe that learning is innate and fixed rather than acquired and elastic. Many believe in multi-tasking, that they can learn while simultaneously attending to other matters, ignoring the plain limit of cognitive load. Many see knowledge as memorized, isolated facts rather than integrated frameworks acquiring meaning primarily when applied.

Coaching students in better attitudes may help some, although the studies showing persistence of wrong attitudes suggest not much help. Methods may be more effective, like requiring multiple drafts of work before final submission, requiring review exercises, and building practice performances into instruction. Encouraging study plans and journals, and self-assessment of study habits and learning progress, can help improve mindset. Address directly issues of fear and mistrust. Exercises that require reflection and analysis, and that space and interleave topic study, may help form reflective and evaluative habits. Counteract poor attitude using methods more than exhortation. And enjoy the week.
Nelson

Enhancing Classroom Instruction No. 154: Problems with Learning
[Research] [04/02/20]

Good morning, professors. Please consider this brief note about six problems that students encounter in learning, and six remedies, drawn from Professors Engelmann and Carnine's text *Theory of Instruction*. You'll likely recognize all six problems:

1. The first problem is when students don't transfer learning from the practice context to the final context. They practice well but perform poorly. The remedy is to approximate the practice context closer to the final context. Make the exercise more like the measured test;

2. A second problem arises when students don't distinguish knowledge applications. They apply new knowledge in wrong situations. The remedy is to instruct in the discrimination (explain it) while supplying more discrimination practice with closer non-examples;

3. A third problem arises when students don't follow task instructions because they differ from prior instructions. They do what they did previously rather than follow new instructions. The remedy is to distinguish (explain) instructions while approximating practice instructions to final instructions;

4. A fourth problem involves students not being able to perform in the new context. They know the new concept but can't use it. The solution is to adjust practice context to more closely approximate final context;

5. A fifth problem involves students who cannot perform as the task's instructions require. They recognize that the new concept applies to the context but cannot apply it properly. Here, the remedy is to shape (guide and coach in) the response that the task requires;

6. A final problem involves students simply not trying at all. They make no effort rather than an erring effort. Here, the solution is to induce students to do what challenges them less, several times in succession, before re-introducing the challenging task. Reduce the behavioral obstacle until students are ready to perform it.

The distinctions are subtle, but the first three problems above involve issues with the stimuli, while the last three problems above involve issues with the student. Both stimuli and students matter. Sometimes you need to fix instructional stimuli. Sometimes you need to apply different methods. Enjoy the last of the week.

Nelson

Enhancing Classroom Instruction No. 155: Discerning the Principles
[Methods] [04/03/20]
Good morning, professors. Please consider this brief note about the importance of discerning *why* your methods (especially new methods) work, discerning the *proven principle* behind them, rather than simply adopting and persisting with certain practices. Your practices may be less important than the principles that guide, verify, and vitalize them.

See, for instance, if your new method poses *desirable difficulties* in the student's zone of proximal development. Or maybe your method draws on *test-enhanced learning*, in which students learn from the test itself. Or perhaps the *generation effect*, in which students infer and create content, supplies the method's positive effects. Or the method may be facilitating *retrieval practice* or promoting students' *self-explanations*. Or your new method may be requiring *distributed practice* or helping students to *interleave* their studies. Or you may be setting up an *expertise-reversal effect* in which students acquire and exercise the expertise. Your method may entail *worked examples* engaging them in concept application, demonstrate the *coherence principle*, or depend on *elaborative interrogation*.

Behavioral psychologists have identified, tested, and proven the value of these principles, demonstrating their positive effects. Apply this science of learning to your instruction. Test your methods for their proven principles producing your desired learning effect. And enjoy the weekend.
Nelson

Enhancing Classroom Instruction No. 156: The Challenge of Change
[Morale] [04/06/20]
Good morning, professors. In this peculiarly chaotic moment, please consider this brief note regarding the challenges of change. Change challenges organizations and the front-line personnel who must implement it. Organizations systematize to help the organization persist, just as we routinize and repeat practices. System changes and changes to routines feel like threats to organizational security and personal value.

Vision can spur, accelerate, enhance, and preserve change. But implementation requires investment, especially front-line-personnel personal investment. That's us. No change will happen without our commitment, effort, work drive--the qualities that we urge on students but must adopt and hone ourselves. Change also requires assessment and the modification or confirmation that follows assessment.

Change also depends on supportive culture. Discouraging reformers retards change. Enhancing instruction takes courage and energy. The easiest thing to do today is what you did yesterday. Change feels chaotic. Its principles are simple and orderly, but its process is complex, shifting. One change affects the whole system of instruction. Expect chaotic responses. Face them with poise and determination. And enjoy this week of extraordinary opportunity. Crises, external or internal, are not to waste.

Nelson

Enhancing Classroom Instruction No. 157: Professional Learning

[Morale] [04/07/20]

Good morning, professors. In a reflective moment today, see if you experience the three challenges that Professor Bradley in *Designing Organizations for Meaningful Professional Learning* discerns for professional learning.

Professors first face the technical challenge of getting right the instructional enhancements, a considerable challenge given how complex and fluid instruction is. Fortunately, law professors have extraordinary skills for acquiring technical knowledge, meaning that we need only shift that skill to acquire instructional knowledge, not just subject knowledge.

The greater challenge to professional change may be emotional. Teaching takes confidence. Implementing instructional enhancements removes the familiarity and comfort from which confidence comes. Professors rightly question whether they will master what they need and whether they have enough control to make change work. Recognize your need to deal with reactive emotions.

A third challenge involves unintentionally shifting organizational hierarchies and social relationships within the school. Enhancements can come from anywhere, not solely the usual sanctioned source. Senior

professors who accept enhancements that junior colleagues promote may relinquish hard-earned standing. Don't underestimate the social challenges to change. Admit what you must, and move forward dealing with it adroitly. Enjoy the week.
Nelson

Enhancing Classroom Instruction No. 158: A Few Good Questions
[Morale] [04/08/20]
Good morning, professors. Please consider these few good questions to re-stimulate your interest in enhancing instruction. I don't know about you, but I need frequent refreshers and re-starters.

First, keep asking yourself *what you want students to be able to do*. You are a discipline expert with considerable teaching experience. You know what you want instruction to achieve and problems students have in achieving it. Behavioral outcomes focus you on methods for achievement.

Second, ask *where students make the most mistakes* and *what students get wrong*. These questions help you focus on influencing and correcting observable behaviors. Third, ask *why your subject matters*, including *how you got into the field*. These questions highlight values you may wish to communicate along with your subject's knowledge and skills.

Let these questions help you discern differences between what you want students to achieve and the methods you must use to help them achieve it. Although we are law experts, learning more about law within our field may not make us better professors. We may instead need to learn more about influencing student behavior. Enjoy the rest of the week.
Nelson

Enhancing Classroom Instruction No. 159: Change Principles
[Morale] [04/09/20]
Good morning, professors. Please consider these principles when pursuing, implementing, and evaluating instructional changes.

First, focus on results. As much as designs can contribute to improving instruction, the methods are not the point. The results remain the point. If you can't design in ways to measure results, then reconsider the change.

Second, consider everything affecting teaching including time and resource constraints, and competing demands on both you and students. We do not work in a vacuum, and students don't study in vacuums. Change affects other things.

Third, make changes that add value. Do not change simply for the sake of change or to affect outcomes that have little or no significance. Direct changes to outcomes that need improvement.

Fourth, work collaboratively. Two heads are better than one. Even as you discern what you believe is best, listen to others, and share with others. The work and views of others may accelerate your changes exponentially.

Finally, remain neutral as to the advocate and form of solutions. The goal is to succeed, not to succeed only through certain persons, means, or methods. The best changes sometimes come from sources and in forms you wouldn't expect.

I hope you see some wisdom in these principles for change. Enjoy the last of the week and term.
Nelson

Enhancing Classroom Instruction No. 160: Evidence-Based Practices
[Research] [04/10/20]
Good morning, professors. Please consider this last note of the term, urging that we continue to research and use evidence-based practices to enhance instruction.

Professors train and work in a practice-based, rather than evidence-based, culture. Yet Professor Maheady and co-authors in the chapter *EBP in Teacher Preparation* advocate that we can, should, and perhaps must ground our work in scientific research. Accreditation standards require that professors define outcomes and assess instruction against those outcomes in evidence-based manner. And why shouldn't we do so, the edicts of our federal overlords aside?

While some teaching practices have empirical support, many do not. Some practices slow rather than speed learning. Science-supported research tests practices and their enhancements, gathering and evaluating evidence of their impact. We have evidence-based opportunities. The challenge is in building our shared competence in their research and use.

Use wisely your reflective and preparation time over the break and into the next term, with the engagement and excitement that the following scenario suggests. Enjoy the break.
Nelson

While the professor was teaching, the librarian had delivered another stack of books on applied behavior analysis to her office. The professor looked at the stack in satisfaction. She knew that within a couple or few days, the books would be gone, read or reviewed and returned to the library for shipping back to their home libraries. The professor delighted in the facility with which the library obtained new and old texts, enabling her to explore other fields deeply with little more than an email request to her reference librarian. The professor gleaned only a thought or two from some texts, while other texts offered copious insights. But the excitement of the book stacks was exactly that exploration: one never quite knew what one would discover.

Part II

Online Instruction

Enhancing Online Instruction No. 1: Sharing Whiteboards
[Methods] [05/04/20]
Good morning, professors. Please consider this brief note about how to use a shared whiteboard to increase student engagement during an online class. While online classes eliminate the opportunity for in-person paired and small-group work, in other ways they increase opportunities for student group engagement.

To give students opportunities for online in-class group engagement, create a Google Doc in your Google Drive course folder. Title the doc "Whiteboard--Paired." Write pairs of student names down the Whiteboard's left-hand side, leaving a few rows between pairs for the paired students to work. Then, just before class, prepare to share the Whiteboard with full read/write rights with all students in the class. Click the "include file in email" box to ease student access.

When the moment comes in class when you want students to work in pairs using the Whiteboard, when for instance you pose a designed question of recall, illustration, or, better yet, application to the class, toggle on your shared screen to send the Whiteboard to the students, telling and showing them that it is in their gmail inbox and to open it and work on the answer in the designated pairs.

Then, sit back and watch the paired students work. Watching collaborative written work is fascinating. Keep your student groups to just two or three at most, or you will get holdouts who do not participate and excellers who dominate. When the answers are mostly finished, share your encouragement and guidance with the class, although students will have likely already self-assessed simply by watching other pairs work. Thank you, and enjoy the term.
Nelson

Enhancing Online Instruction No. 2: More Whiteboards
[Methods] [05/05/20]
Good morning, professors. Please consider this brief note describing another way to use whiteboards in class to promote student engagement, this time individually. You would probably never do this activity in an in-person class, but it is easy in an online class.

Create a Google Sheet in your Google Drive folder for your course. Title the sheet "Whiteboard--Individual." In the sheet, list your students down the first column. Title each successive column Activity 1, Activity 2, etc. Then, just before class, prepare to share the sheet with all students in class, granting them full read/write rights. Include the sheet in the gmail (check that box in the share menu) for ease of student access.

When time comes in class for students to use the individual whiteboard, such as to answer your question of recall, illustration, or best yet application, toggle from your shared Webex screen to your Whiteboard—Individual file, and hit send. Tell students to answer in the Activity 1 box next to their name. If you grow concerned about students misusing someone else's response box, then in the sheet grant permission for each row for only the student named.

Watch in class as students answer. You will see which students answer promptly and correctly, and which students depend on notes, other research, or watching classmates to answer. Any effort, though, helps, even wrong-answer efforts. You can then share your encouragement and guidance. You will also notice students correcting their answers, which is fine. Remember, some studies show that wrong answers are just about as good as right answers if corrected promptly. Enjoy the day.
Nelson

Enhancing Online Instruction No. 3: Designed Questions
[Methods] [05/06/20]
Good morning, professors. Please accept this brief note about how to prepare questions before class for students to answer online at specific points in class, to increase engagement and provide instant assessment and feedback.

In your Google Drive folder for your course, create a Google Form, titling it Week 1 In-Class Survey. Examine your slide show for the best moments to pose a question for each student in the online class to promptly answer using the form. Vary the question forms among checkboxes and short answer. If you use multiple choice, then include an "Other" option to encourage student engagement. Multiple choice, true/false, and other one-right-option questions reduce student effort.

Prepare to share the form when class starts, telling students when class starts that you have just shared the form. Include the form in your email (check that sharing box) for ease of student access. Then, when you reach that point in lecture or discussion, toggle in your shared Webex screen to the form, point out the question students are to answer, and tell them to hit "submit" when they do so. Watch student responses accumulate one by one until most students have answered. Then show the pie chart or other data on the answers, sharing your guidance and encouragement. Enjoy the rest of the week.
Nelson

Enhancing Online Instruction No. 4: Whiteboard Questions
[Methods] [05/07/20]
Good morning, professors. Please accept this brief note about how to use your online-class shared whiteboard to design questions in advance to pose at strategic points during lecture and discussion.

A prior message this week suggested how to use a shared Google Doc as a whiteboard on which all students can work in pairs for your review and class evaluation. You would pose an audio question in class for students to answer in writing on the whiteboard, working in their designated space on the whiteboard in their designated pairs.

Some students, though, will not have heard or will have misunderstood your audio question, and thus will struggle answering on the whiteboard. They may need to refer to your question repeatedly while answering. You may also not have been sufficiently clear in your question. To address these shortcomings, write your anticipated questions on the whiteboard above the student pairs before class.

As yesterday's message indicated, you may prefer to use a Google Form with your designed questions and one of the Form's standard formats (multiple choice, checkboxes, short answer, paragraph answer, etc.). But if you like the open-format whiteboard and yet want the structure of a designed question, then write the question in advance on the whiteboard. I have used both forums (a whiteboard and a form) in a single online class, which works, although can also be a little cumbersome. Enjoy the rest of the week.
Nelson

Enhancing Online Instruction No. 5: Building Class Morale
[Methods] [05/08/20]
Good morning, professors. Please accept this brief note on how to build and assess online class morale using a Google Form at the beginning and end of classes. Just because students are physically separate from one another does not mean that they can't share their individual and collective mood, and build a class morale, as they would do at an in-person class before and after class.

Return to the weekly Google Form that you created to pose content and application questions at strategic points in your lecture or discussion. In that form, add a first and last question raising social, mood, attitudinal, and other morale issues. For instance, if your class is facing an extraordinary, globe-encircling pandemic that has for the first time in history shuttered their economy and isolated them at home, then have the first question ask how they are doing.

Rather than asking an open-ended question that might elicit personal detail and burden the class, consider a multiple-choice question the options of which are collectively frank, authentic, humorous, and guiding in encouraging student resolve. When you share the form, be sure not to collect student emails revealing respondent identity (an option you'd have to choose--the default is not to collect). Show the class their collective responses, so that they see how one another is doing. Comment positively and helpfully on those responses, such as admitting that you are feeling the same way, too (all options).

For the last question of the class, ask something that points them forward resolutely. Here may be where you'd prefer to ask an open-ended (short-answer or paragraph-answer) question. For instance, ask them what they need to best prepare for an upcoming exam or assignment. Ask them if they have any ideas how to help one another study or otherwise navigate issues they may face at that point in the term. Watch their responses as they write in their form, but don't show those responses unless you judge them helpful. You may wish to end the class with the question and review responses after class, sharing after class in email or other form what you feel is most helpful. Enjoy the rest of the week.
Nelson

Enhancing Online Instruction No. 6: Supporting the Back Channel
[Methods] [05/11/20]
Good morning, professors. Please accept this brief note about supporting the back channel in your online class. In-person classes have important back channels. Help your online students use their online back channel to increase engagement and supply assessment and instant feedback. The Webex meeting with which you conduct online class has a chat function. You have seen it and likely used it. Here are some obvious and less-obvious uses for it.

The chat function is obviously useful for students to alert you about class problems (microphones off, screen not shared, etc.). Either turn the chat function on so that you can follow it to the right of your screen during class, or at least notice (watch for) the chat pop-ups in the upper-right of your screen, and check the chat dot when alerting you to new content. Don't ignore chat, especially when it involves class transmission issues.

The chat function can also be quite helpful for students to chime in answering your questions, without disrupting the audio flow of the class. Encourage students to answer with a chat or audio, giving them both options. When students do answer with a chat, acknowledge their answer and thank them for contributing, while guiding them (giving feedback) about errant or unhelpful responses, just as you would do in an in-person class.

The chat function can do more, though, than just alert you to student questions, answers, or problems. The chat function has a drop-down menu at its bottom that enables students and you to send chat only to an individual in the class rather than to everyone in the class. Students may use that function to send you a private message. Watch for it, and respond promptly if urgent. You can give a brief, instant response while a student is reciting or answering on the audio channel, without interrupting class.

Students may also chat privately with one another during class. Some professors would wish to discourage that off-line, back-channel chat as distracting and even undermining. But my sense at least in my own classes is that the back channel can perform important functions, allowing students to guide and support one another, even when (especially when) they have issues with the class. If you acknowledge

and support the back channel, you may effectively co-opt it for your instructional goals in the class. Enjoy the weekend.
Nelson

Enhancing Online Instruction No. 7: Drawing on the Back Channel
[Methods] [05/12/20]
Good morning, professors. Please accept this brief note about how to draw on, and thus co-opt and reduce the distraction of, the student back channel during an online class.

One of the challenges of an online class is that all students are viewing a computer screen, where they may have greater-than-ever ability and temptation to surf the internet, do email, send texts, and engage in other non-class-related virtual activities during class. Think of this back-channel issue from a behavioral standpoint. Staring at a computer screen for hours at a time without the reward of interacting with the device is incredibly stressful--an enormous adverse stimulus to paying attention in an online class. Hence, back-channel activities, simply to ease the stress.

To meet this challenge, consider engaging the back channel. When, for instance, a question arises about a data point, as they often do in class, and no one seems to have the answer in audio or chat, invite students to search for the answer (only if it is a quick, not a deep-research, answer). Here's an illustration that commonly arises in torts classes. An older case opinion shares that the award was X dollars. Translating those dollars to today's dollar values takes some intuitive skill. The *NY Times v Sullivan* award in the early 1960s was just $500,000. But that's millions of today dollars.

Inviting students to quickly find an online amortization tool to tell the class (best by chat, for you to acknowledge audibly) the amortized value informs the class, teaches a quick-research skill, and eases the device-constraint stress for the student who pursues it. Few do, but those who do appreciate the invite. Co-opting the back channel gives students permission to ease their stress but in an engaging, useful, informative, and skill-building manner. Enjoy the week.
Nelson

Enhancing Online Instruction No. 8: Breakout Chats
[Methods] [05/13/20]
Good morning, professors. Please accept this brief note about how to support mini-breakout sessions using Webex's private-chat function.

One of the harder things to engineer in online instruction is breakout work between pairs or small groups of students. Communications tend to flow through the whole class, limiting the ability of students to experiment and build confidence in private pairs. Some students just won't put forth effort out of fear of embarrassment and failure before the class.

Yet you've already seen that Webex's chat function allows meeting participants to direct private communications between participants, not just to the whole meeting group. This private-chat function means that when you assign students to work in pairs on a whiteboard file shared with the whole class, those pairs have the opportunity to use the chat function to communicate privately about their work.

Encourage students to use the private-chat function to pose questions to one another, to correct or question one another's work, or to otherwise evaluate, assess, and support. Help students help one another, even in this constrained virtual environment. Enjoy the rest of the week.
Nelson

Enhancing Online Instruction No. 9: Out-of-Class Resources
[Resources] [05/14/20]
Good morning, professors. Please accept this brief note about out-of-class resources for online (remote) instruction. Managing a remote class in Webex to engage students and maximize learning is one skill, one activity. But how does that in-class online work relate to out-of-class resources? Should we be redesigning or reorganizing our out-of-class resources when shifting from in-person to online instruction?

In one sense, out-of-class resources for an online (remote) class may be the same for in-person classroom instruction. Class is class, whether in person or online, served by the same resources. We may not need to redesign or restructure anything when moving from in-person to online instruction.

Yet engaging students solely through a computer-screen interface seems somehow to warrant altering other resources. If class engages students online, forcing all students into the virtual environment, then out-of-class resources may better link with that same virtual environment. Online class may work better if it connects students with other enhanced online resources. Let's explore that premise together. Watch for upcoming messages. Enjoy the rest of the week.
Nelson

Enhancing Online Instruction No. 10: Embedding Quizzes
[Resources] [05/15/20]
Good morning, professors. Please accept this brief note about the value of embedding quizzes in flipped-classroom online lectures.

You know how easy Canvas's Studio makes embedding questions in your flipped-classroom online lectures. You can easily insert questions every couple of minutes in your ten- to twenty-minute summary slide-show-backed lectures in your weekly Canvas resources. Doubling your lecture speed using the settings halves the time you need take to discern where to insert your questions.

Studio's three question formats, multiple choice, true/false, and multiple answer, are each helpful formats for different levels of engagement. True/false can quickly confirm a key point. Multiple choice can supply prompt application. And multiple answer can help students recall, list, and sort elements, criteria, factors, or conditions. Don't miss the value of these questions. Studies have shown how the least bit of back-and-forth engagement during a presentation can enhance recall. More-effortful engagement enhances understanding and application.

Shifting to all-online instruction this term, I added quiz questions to all my weekly flipped-classroom slide-show lectures to give students greater opportunity to engage and test their learning. Those lectures were already a favorite student resource. They should now be a more-effective resource for their learning. Enjoy the weekend.
Nelson

Enhancing Online Instruction No. 11: Organizing Resources
[Resources] [05/18/20]

Good morning, professors. Please accept this brief note about organizing online resources. One of the challenges to all-online instruction is that it intensifies the virtual environment's use, making its organization all the more important.

Organization of the online environment is key to access. Students won't use resources that they can't locate readily and consistently. They also won't see the integrative value of those resources if their virtual connections are unclear. If they don't see framework and sense value, then they won't use those resources or will lose some confidence in them and thus benefit less from them.

Canvas has its organizational strengths and weaknesses in expressing clear organization for improved access. Its great weakness is that it does not enable professors to label the primary navigation links to the left of the home course page. You get traditional choices like Assignments and Quizzes, and the wonky Modules. You don't get Exam Resources or Flipped Lectures, although you can create these content areas under Modules.

What Canvas does do well, though, is enable links to resources. Thus, to maximize visual navigation from the home page, you can create a table of contents that has direct links to various weekly resources. For example, you can help students click directly to your Week 4 flipped-classroom lecture with embedded quiz, from the home page. You can link assignments to quizzes to modules, creating both visual structure and ready navigation.

Canvas is not particularly intuitive. It has taken me hours of research through poorly written, overly technical explanations, and much experimentation, just to accomplish relatively simple things. Yet with effort, you can make it a reasonably organized, visual, and accessible home for resources. Use Canvas's strengths, and remediate its weaknesses. And enjoy the week.
Nelson

Enhancing Online Instruction No. 12: The Difference with Online
[Methods] [05/19/20]
Good morning, professors. Please accept this brief note about a difference between online and classroom instruction. Learning means to

change behavior in a way that persists. Instruction should foster that change and its persistence. How does online instruction differ in these fundamentals from classroom instruction?

Perhaps the two forums do not differ in their fundamentals. Whether teaching in the classroom or online, we still offer stimuli, rehearsal, reward, and spaced repetition, the very things that support persistent behavioral change. Importantly, *the principles do not change.* Virtual forums have no magic to them, whether Canvas, Webex, Panopto, Studio, Blackboard, CALI, Quizlet, TWEN, or the sure-to-come next iteration.

What is different about remote instruction is that every student is now devotedly on computer during class time. *Every student thus has a way to respond to every inquiry at the same time.* This one opportunity, to invoke precise written responses from all students at the same time, or from many students at once, may be the primary opportunity to pursue.

Chat and shared Google Forms, Docs, and Sheets, are a few ways to foster, process, and display in real time mass student responses, engaging all students at once in a designed manner. We have a great opportunity. Let's seize it. Enjoy the week.
Nelson

Enhancing Online Instruction No. 13: Knowing Your Online Learner
[Research] [05/20/20]
Good morning, professors. Please consider this brief note drawn from educational psychologist and online curriculum designer Tina Stavredes's book *Effective Online Teaching,* advocating that we who teach online should first know these key attributes of our adult online learners:

1. *need to know why* they must learn what you are asking them to learn;
2. *strong self-concept* resisting learning that requires altering self-concept;
3. *substantial experience* on which they need and want to draw;
4. *readiness to learn* when having problems to solve;
5. *internal motivation* to learn, like job satisfaction and quality of life.

Online instruction is not all about technologies and methods. Online instruction, like other instruction, is about fitting instruction to learner attributes. Show your adult online learners why they need to know and how knowing enhances their existing identity, connects with their experience, solves real problems, and improves their life. Enjoy the rest of the week.

Nelson

Enhancing Online Instruction No. 14: Social Presence/Introductions
[Methods] [05/21/20]
Good morning, professors. Please accept this brief note about helping online students exhibit social presence, using introduction exercises.

Research summarized in *A Guide to Online Course Design* suggests that social presence is key to retaining online students at high engagement levels. But how do you support social presence?

One way is to share a table like the one at this link that allows students to disclose ambitions, dreams, affinities, and other information of your choice. You decide how professional or personal, serious or silly to make the inquiries.

As you can see from this example, students can share as much or as little personal, professional, or other information as they choose, following your guide. Students can also see what one another shares.

You can further your relationship with each student by sending periodic individual messages to students with career, networking, and other tips and encouragement. Help students show social presence online. And enjoy the last of the week.

Nelson

Enhancing Online Instruction No. 15: Persistence Problems
[Research] [05/22/20]
Good morning, professors. Please accept this brief note drawn from Dr. Stavredes's *Effective Online Teaching*, summarizing persistence problems that online learners exhibit more so than learners in traditional classrooms. We don't want to lose students this summer because of online-only instruction.

Retention models for traditional classroom instruction of college-age students tend to focus on social support and program integration of students. In that traditional model, relationships fostering commitment to the institution matter.

Retention models for non-traditional, remote, adult instruction more like our current circumstances focus instead on student-institution fit, recognizing that external factors like jobs, finances, and family influence online persistence to a greater degree than in traditional programs.

Thus, the retention key for adult online learners is less social/integrative and more academic/psychological. Are students sensing that they are progressing, learning, acquiring useful knowledge and skills? Are your designs efficient, well-organized, clear, and sound enough to support that learning?

When students cannot integrate socially, they depend more than ever on your sensitive, productive, just-in-time designs. Reduce frustration, increase efficacy. And enjoy the weekend.
Nelson

Enhancing Online Instruction No. 16: Factors Practice
[Methods] [05/25/20]
Good morning, professors. Please accept this brief note on an easy way to get frequent guided student practice applying factors or making other written applications in an online course.

Law has many multi-factor tests. Students must learn, recall, and apply a list of factors, involving issue spotting, memory, reasoning, and writing skills. Learning the factors is one skill, while applying them quickly and sensibly is another skill.

To increase student guided practice in an online course, create a Google shared sheet like this example. After presenting instruction on the multi-factor test, direct students to the shared file, asking them to generate an example application on the line next to their name, like the model application at the form's top. Notice that this form offers the students a rubric for a strong answer. If you prefer, you can give students multiple scenarios to which to apply the factors, like this second example.

Then watch the shared file as students work. You may notice students taking cues from the work of other students, which is fine if they are stuck. As students finish, you can laud individual examples or the whole class's work, or point out pattern defects that you see in the work. Practice, practice, practice, right? Enjoy the week.
Nelson

Enhancing Online Instruction No. 17: Scaffolding Support
[Research [05/26/20]
Good morning, professors. Please consider this brief note drawn from Dr. Stavredes's *Effective Online Teaching* about how graphic organizers can help online learners.

You might recall yesterday's note that field-dependent learners, those who do not readily separate new items from their context, tend to misunderstand and confuse those new items, but that concept scaffolding can help. Graphic organizers are one way to help students scaffold (both connect and disconnect) new items.

Graphic organizers can include flow charts, organization charts, concept maps, spider maps, idea trees, comparison charts, venn diagrams, cycle diagrams, and event series. See the Google Images search at this link, or search for the specific form that you think might most work. When you elaborate the knowledge into graphic form, you help students create additional retrieval routes (meaning, recall better).

Look at your slideshows and resources: are they just long lists of information, or are you sharing graphic organizers? Consider helping students scaffold by using graphic organizers, especially in the highly distractible, chaotic online environment. And enjoy the week.
Nelson

Enhancing Online Instruction No. 18: Cognitive Presence
[Research] [05/27/20]
Good morning, professors. Please consider this brief note drawn from Dr. Stavredes's *Effective Online Teaching* about using active-learning strategies to promote online *cognitive presence*. A greater challenge for

online learners over classroom learners is simply to mentally attend to (concentrate, follow, track) what is going on in the class session.

Physical classroom presence tends to capture mental classroom presence because instructors and learners can see, and thus hold accountable, one another. By contrast, virtual instruction captures at most only a few learners' faces, leaving the learners largely anonymous, reducing accountability, and letting learners check out and hide.

Critical-thinking approaches help regain cognitive presence. Challenge students to be clear, accurate, precise, relevant, deep, broad, logical, significant, and fair in their surmises. Problem-based approaches, and argument/counter-argument methods, can also help. Generally, active-learning strategies that engage students are the better course, but make those activities critical and deep, not just rote. And enjoy the rest of the week.
Nelson

Enhancing Online Instruction No. 19: Supporting Critical Thinking
[Research] [05/28/20]
Good morning, professors. Please consider this brief note drawn from Dr. Stavredes's *Effective Online Teaching* about supporting and modeling critical thinking for online learners.

We know that critical thinking is both necessary for effective law practice (not to mention bar passage) and also key to promoting greater learning. What, though, is critical thinking? One model suggests that critical thinking has these eight dimensions:

1. *point of view*, wherein the learner considers alternative perspectives;
2. *purpose*, wherein the learner identifies and hews to the thought's goal;
3. *question*, wherein the learner identifies the precise issue to address;
4. *information*, wherein the learner discerns the data necessary to decide;
5. *inference*, wherein the learner considers alternative interpretations to draw;
6. *concepts*, wherein the learner identifies and defines applicable concepts;
7. *assumptions*, wherein the learner recognizes and tests hypotheses; and
8. *implications*, wherein the learner considers impacts from conclusions.

Prepare to pose online questions and structure online problem solving and discussion that fosters critical thinking in its above several dimensions. And enjoy the rest of the week.
Nelson

Enhancing Online Instruction No. 20: Virtual Collaboration
[Research] [05/29/20]
Good morning, professors. Please consider this brief note drawn from Dr. Stavredes's *Effective Online Teaching* about how to ensure that virtual teamwork, projects, and collaborations are successful in achieving learning goals. We've all had the experience of launching student team projects and seeing them succeed or fail. Why, though, do some succeed while others flounder?

Sound virtual team projects generally have these elements: (1) clearly defined participant roles; (2) clear time limits; (3) clear guides for how teams are to proceed or decide (by unanimity, consensus, or individually as to roles); (4) clear guides for how to treat non-participating members; and (5) some flexibility in choice of team, participant role, performance time, or time demands.

Sound virtual team projects generally also require the instructor to play these roles: (1) setting the stage as above, including learning outcomes; (2) creating the environment (preparing materials, scheduling breakout rooms, etc.); (3) modeling performance in participant interactions (i.e., doing as you expect students to do); (4) monitoring the process to ensure appropriate progress; and (5) evaluating the process at conclusion for appropriate follow up.

Next time we plan a virtual collaboration for students, let's be sure to do more than throw the figurative ball out there to see what happens. Ensure you are considering each element and fulfilling each instructor role. And enjoy the weekend.
Nelson

Enhancing Online Instruction No. 21: Cognitive Distortions
[Research] [06/01/20]
Good morning, professors. From the virus crisis and other stressors, you may notice unhealthy cognitive distortion among your students.

145

Challenges, even crises, can produce phenomenal growth and strength in individuals and organizations... with a sound mindset. Here are some cognitive-behavioral-therapy tips you may consider sharing with students to improve crisis mindset:

1. Don't let emotions color reality. Just because you feel down doesn't mean things aren't working for you. You can feel down but have things going great;
2. Don't catastrophize events, focusing on the worst possible outcome. Worst-possible outcomes are by definition unlikely;
3. Don't overgeneralize events, assuming one negative means everything's negative. One negative is just one negative;
4. Don't dichotomize thinking. Everything isn't all or nothing. Just about everything is instead somewhere in between;
5. Don't label inappropriately and negatively. Neither you nor the one with whom or thing with which you are interacting is that simple;
6. Avoid mind reading, assuming the worst intentions. You may not know the other's motivation and intent until you ask and find out. It's likely not all about you, anyway;
7. Don't filter only for negative data. Data is generally some good, some bad. See the good along with the bad;
8. Don't diminish the positives. Even difficult, generally bad situations have some positives, even strong positives. See and value the positives.

I hope these thoughts give you some ideas for how to help students cope, and indeed, how to cope yourself. Things ain't easy right now, but somehow, we trust that they are nonetheless working in our favor. Enjoy the week.
Nelson

Enhancing Online Instruction No. 22: Instructor-Student Interactions
[Research] [06/02/20]
Good morning, professors. Please accept these brief recommendations from Dr. Stavredes's *Effective Online Teaching* on how to use your interactions with students online to promote critical thinking.

The impersonal, virtual nature of online forums can discourage reflective discussion. Whether your interactions are in online audio discussions, written discussion groups, written questions, polls and surveys, or otherwise, deepen reflection and model critical thinking using these question forms:

1. to get discussion started when students hesitate, use *prompts* restating or clarifying the question, or suggesting a possible answer;
2. to amplify and deepen discussion when comments are sound but basic, request *elaboration* of responses;
3. to address unclear or confusing responses, request *clarification* of underlying logic, rule, or reasoning;
4. to move discussion forward, *synthesize* responses around patterns, while raising new questions;
5. to extend limited discussion, seek alternative *perspectives* such as asking students to assume or change roles;
6. to reveal underlying logic, ask students to share *inferences* and *assumptions* underlying their responses;
7. to demonstrate discussion's significance, ask for *implications* of the conclusions students have drawn; and
8. to conclude discussion, ask for *summaries* of discussion points that prioritize concept value.

These recommendations would apply equally in the classroom but seem especially important to foster deeper online discussion, where simply communicating at all seems an achievement. It's not. The achievement is learning to think critically. Focus on that outcome over the technological mastery of communication media. And enjoy the week.
Nelson

Enhancing Online Instruction No. 23: Online-Interaction Guidelines
[Research] [06/03/20]
Good morning, professors. Please accept this brief note from Dr. Stavredes's *Effective Online Teaching* on guidelines for positive online communication.

We all know how easy misunderstanding virtual communications is and how the impersonal virtual environment can foster abusive communication. To avoid misunderstanding and abuses, follow and promote these guidelines:

1. Think of the person or persons receiving the communication;
2. Post nothing that you would not say to the person's face, in person;

3. Conduct yourself virtually as you would in person, meaning with integrity;
4. Respect recipient time and attention, avoiding wasteful communication;
5. Appearance (grammar, spelling, format) counts virtually as in person;
6. Prepare for online forums as you would for in-person meetings;
7. Help or guide to help students or others who have issues or questions;
8. Do not start online disputes or fuel disputes, as they are hard to end;
9. Forgive mistakes quickly, while being patient and compassionate.

In short, humanize this inhuman virtual environment. Don't let it change your spirit and soul. Let your spirit and soul saturate it with personality, care, compassion, and commitment, modeling that professional conduct for students. Enjoy the rest of the week.
Nelson

Enhancing Online Instruction No. 24: Keys to Online Success
[Research] [06/04/20]
Good morning, professors. Please accept this brief note drawn from the book *Lessons from the Virtual Classroom* by two organizational developers, about several keys to online-instruction success.

We must first manage the technology, which isn't the answer to anything but yet the vital medium--not the message but still the medium, like finding your way to the right classroom. Instructors then need to develop reliable procedures conducive to learning, or you'll have angry, disappointed, and disaffected students.

Then, instructors need to design for higher levels of engagement. Just being technically savvy and procedurally fair and efficient isn't enough, if students aren't participating in ways that help them practice meeting instructional goals. Somewhere in that design mix, we also hope to foster collaboration, teamwork, and social support and development.

Finally, instructors should promote student reflection over their learning, encouraging skill development and attitude adjustment toward self-directed learning. We, too, need to reflect. As you continue to dive into online instruction, see how you're doing on each of these keys to success. And enjoy the last of the week.
Nelson

Enhancing Online Instruction No. 25: Assessment Corrections
[Assessment] [06/05/20]
Good morning, professors. Please accept this brief note sharing a way to engage students collectively in feedback on their assessments. We all see error patterns in our evaluation of student performance. How do we best share that feedback with students?

While individual scoring rubrics can serve individual students remarkably well in correcting individual errors, students can also learn from the errors of other students, affirming their correct performance and ensuring that they retain and amplify those performances.

After your next interim exam or other student work product, try creating a Google Sheet like this one organizing the most-common errors with their corrections. Share the file in class, asking students to read each error and commit (check the box) to any correction they especially hope to follow.

With each successive exam or other work product, add errors and corrections to the same file, asking for further student commitments. Let all students learn from one another's errors, and show them their collective progress. And enjoy the weekend.
Nelson

Enhancing Online Instruction No. 26: Anticipating Rewards
[Methods] [06/08/20]
Good morning, professors. Please accept this brief note suggesting a way to help students connect distant career rewards toward which they may be working, with their present practices. We know that the distance of reinforcement from long-term career rewards presents a problem to shaping present student study behaviors. Here's a thought for addressing that disconnect.

List in a shared file like this one, the top twenty achievements that you may have desired or believe your students may desire in a law career. Then, when students perform especially well in class, whether singly, in groups, or as a class, encourage them to select a reward. Sure, the selected rewards are only virtual, imaginary, but they can remind students of that for which they work.

Reflecting over and selecting possible rewards of a law career can also remind students of career opportunities and help them reflect on their own commitments and identity. You'll see, for instance, that I included two desultory addictions among the other positive choices, for each of which I can tell a story of lawyers whom I knew who made those unfortunate choices. Let students suggest other rewards to add to your list. Nothing wrong with sharing ambitions. Enjoy the week.
Nelson

Enhancing Online Instruction No. 27: Group Development Online
[Methods] [06/09/20]
Good morning, professors. Please accept this brief note about a method for helping students practice critical thinking. Last week one of these messages described eight ways that students can deepen their critical thinking. We've all seen shallow reasoning and hope to deepen it. Here is a method for helping students practice.

List the eight ways to improve critical thinking on the left-hand column of a Google Sheet file like this one. Across the top of each column to the right, list each student in the class. Begin the first column with an example of those eight critical analyses, for your specific class topic. Share the file during class, challenging students to generate their own examples.

You can watch students in class as they strive to generate examples, some roughly copying other students, while others asking questions or leaving incomplete some of the eight ways. That's all fine. The point is the demonstration, challenge, and effort. Enjoy the week.
Nelson

Enhancing Online Instruction No. 28: Myths to Online Learning
[Research] [06/10/20]
Good morning, professors. Please accept this brief note drawn from Palloff and Pratt's *Lessons from the Virtual Classroom* about these several unhelpful myths that persist about online learning:

1. *Classrooms offer higher-quality instruction than remote learning,* when to the contrary instruction's quality depends much more on other factors;

2. *Online instruction reduces professor-student interaction,* when to the contrary well-designed online courses can maintain or increase interaction;

3. *Employers value classroom degrees more than online degrees,* when to the contrary employers increasingly recognize value in efficient learning;

4. *Professors are less important to online learning,* when to the contrary the instructor's presence, activity, and design is at least as important; and

5. *Online degrees are easier to earn than traditional degrees,* when to the contrary online learning can require greater time, effort, and performance.

Recognize that your remote instruction may be supplying greater value than ever to students. Communicate that belief to students, and they will indeed benefit more from your current work. Enjoy the rest of the week.
Nelson

Enhancing Online Instruction No. 29: Interactive Analyses
[Methods] [06/11/20]
Good morning, professors. Please accept this brief note showing a method to have students practice a sort of interactive analysis in an online class, evaluating their arguments against one another.

List down the left-hand column of a Google Sheet like this one (addressing the elements of fraud) the elements, conditions, factors, or other rule bases for your topic's analysis. Add two columns to the right, one for each side of the argument. Also indicate the names of the students who are to make the analysis on one or another of the rules, on one side or the other.

Share the file in class, asking students to analyze their assigned rule on their assigned side, following a simple fact pattern that you have shared. Designate other students to evaluate the arguments and choose a winner on each rule. Send the winners to your rewards file to select a reward. The exercise lets students make and evaluate arguments and counterarguments. Enjoy the rest of the week.
Nelson

Enhancing Online Instruction No. 30: Navigating Files Online
[Methods] [06/12/20]
Good morning, professors. Please accept this brief note sharing a method for sharing and navigating multiple online interactive files with students for an online class.

We've all had the challenge of toggling back and forth among multiple files to show and share with students in an online synchronous class. Here at this video link is one method for keeping you and students organized and on track. Enjoy the weekend.
Nelson

Enhancing Online Instruction No. 31: Learning Taxonomy
[Research] [06/15/20]
Good morning, professors. Please accept this brief note drawn from *A Guide to Online Course Design* about the forms or categories of learning that online instruction should support.

We readily recognize that online instruction must help students acquire *knowledge*, including terminology, classifications, principles, theories, models, and structures.

Yet online instruction must also help students acquire *skills* including not only steps, techniques, methods, algorithms, heuristics, and protocols, but also metacognitive skills in critical thinking and problem solving.

Finally, online instruction should also help students acquire *dispositions* or *attitudes* including ethics, morals, commitments, affinities, and values.

Don't overlook the varied forms or categories of learning when designing and implementing online instruction. We all know the significance of the knowledge. Can we also share the critical attitudes and skills? Enjoy the week.
Nelson

Enhancing Online Instruction No. 32: Assessment Alternatives
[Assessment] [06/16/20]

Good morning, professors. Please accept this brief note about alternative forms of assessment in an online course. Tests recalling concepts to apply to problems to analyze and justify a solution are not the only assessment form. Consider these other forms:

1. *Performance-based assessments* that test skills like research, drafting, and advocacy, using critical thinking and problem solving to produce real work products like pleadings and other court papers, contracts, articles and bylaws;
2. *Reflective assessments* like journals, blogs, and essays that encourage students to identify their preferred or actual attitudes, values, dispositions, and habits;
3. *Collaborative assessments* like planning litigation or a business acquisition, forming a corporation, or drafting an estate plan, drawing on teamwork skills around a complex project;
4. *Portfolios* collecting, organizing, and displaying student work on a website or social-media site, or in an electronic folder headed by a resume, to share with prospective clients or employers.

Varying assessment forms, even giving students options, can be especially fruitful in online courses, as it engages students more actively and enables greater student sharing and display. Consider alternative assessment, and enjoy the week.
Nelson

Enhancing Online Instruction No. 33: Formative to Summative
[Assessment] [06/17/20]
Good morning, professors. Please accept this brief note about how instructors can move students from formative assessment to summative assessment, which when you think about it is largely instruction's short-term point.

We want students to be able to do things we call *outcomes,* like to deploy critical thinking to make logical arguments adequately supporting propositions convincing specific audiences. And we know the final (summative) assessment: an essay, memorandum, or brief.

Think, though, of the formative assessment forms we can use to bridge students from instruction to summative success. Formative-assessment options include quiz-embedded videos, interim exams, research bibliographies, work-product outlines, written drafts, self-assessments of drafts using guiding rubrics, and peer assessment.

Consider how you relate and link your formative assessments to the final summative work product. Online courses are especially conducive to formative assessment because students are already in the virtual environment where formative assessment often takes place. Enjoy the rest of the week.

Nelson

Enhancing Online Instruction No. 34: Critical-Thinking Models
[Methods] [06/18/20]

Good morning, professors. Please accept this brief note on how to use critical-thinking models to help students develop those skills. We all want students to learn to use sound, logical, rule-based, evidence-based arguments. How, though, do we help students recognize and deploy critical-thinking forms?

Of course, traditional examples, model answers, rubrics, and assessments built around the IRAC construct help. So do exercises that break down the elements of logical argument. For instance, a helpful issue statement should identify the competing interests (the parties), the law construct, and the fact context. Similarly, analyzing a factor requires naming the factor, the party whom it favors, the facts supporting that assertion, and the reasoning why.

Online instruction offers opportunities for students to practice these micro-elements of critical thinking. During class, share a spreadsheet with the students' names down the left column. Then create a column for each element of the logical argument (whether a strong issue statement, a factors analysis, etc.). In the first row, write an example argument meeting all elements. Then tell students to have at it. Watch them write arguments, learning from one another.

Online instruction presents fascinating opportunities for practicing critical-thinking models, at macro and micro levels. Help students build those critical-thinking skills element by element. And enjoy the rest of the week.

Nelson

Enhancing Online Instruction No. 35: Procedural Scaffolding
[Methods] [06/19/20]
Good morning, professors. Please accept this brief note on how to introduce students to the online course's requirements using procedural scaffolding.

One of the challenges to an online course is that course procedure may differ more widely than classroom courses or other online courses. Traditional classroom instruction has traditional procedures: get the syllabus, read the assignment, attend class, take notes, prepare for examination.

Online courses, though, may require other procedures, like starting with an introductory video, perhaps answering questions embedded in the video, then reading to prepare for online practice quizzes, then attending an online class or watching an asynchronous video, followed by completing online exercises.

To help students adjust quickly to unfamiliar online course procedures, make your online course's home page especially clear as to first steps. Prioritize, arrange, and display your course's procedure so that it unfolds logically and clearly to new students. And enjoy the last of the week.
Nelson

Enhancing Online Instruction No. 36: Multimedia Models
[Research] [06/22/20]
Good morning, professors. Please accept this brief note from *A Guide to Online Course Design* summarizing research on effective multimedia presentations in online courses.

Traditional classroom instruction has tended to rely on text-based instructional materials like coursebooks, casebooks, workbooks, articles, and outlines. Online courses instead invite multimedia presentations like video lectures and worked-example demonstrations, given that students are already in the virtual environment. What, though, makes multimedia effective?

First, online students may expect multimedia. Meeting student expectations can alone promote confidence, engagement, and learning.

Second, multimedia naturally supports several forms of dual coding, including text/image, text/animation, narrative/text, and narrative/animation, when dual coding aids learning. Finally, multimedia supports continuity of information, linking information bit to information bit to reduce cognitive load and aid learning.

Examine your online course materials. Place multimedia presentations at key points in your course procedures like introducing units, addressing most-difficult topics, and summarizing or synthesizing topics. And enjoy the week.
Nelson

Enhancing Online Instruction No. 37: Processing Information
[Research] [06/23/20]
Good morning, professors. Please accept this brief note summarizing research models on how learners process information, suggesting principles for online designs.

Instruction begins with sensory stimuli (primarily aural and visual) lasting only moments. Information-processing theory holds that short-term memory retains impressions of those stimuli for about twenty seconds. Short-term memory relates closely to working memory, which involves processing that briefly held information.

Instruction can help learners use short-term memory more productively in working memory, by *chunking and rehearsing the information*, solidifying information bits into recallable and manipulable units. Instruction can then help move short-term, worked memory into long-term memory by *spacing, processing, organizing, and elaborating the information*.

Evaluate your slideshows, diagrams, outlines, lectures, discussions, and other stimuli. Are you chunking and rehearsing information? Then, evaluate your student exercises, problems, reflections, and other engagement activities. Are you helping students space, deep-process, organize, and elaborate learning? Enjoy the rest of the week.
Nelson

Enhancing Online Instruction No. 38: Instructional Strategies
[Research] [06/24/20]
Good morning, professors. Please accept this brief note, drawn from *A Guide to Online Course Design*, suggesting ready ways to vary and deepen your instructional strategies. We aim for relevant instructional outcomes that examination can assess. But how do we coach and trigger practice in those outcomes?

Think simply of the verbs that you choose to direct student performance. If your instructional aim is to show knowledge recall and comprehension, then ask students to *recall, recite, review, identify, articulate,* and *correct.* If your instructional aim is instead application and analysis, then ask students to *apply, assert, address, analyze, solve, prove,* and *explain.*

If your aim is instead to show synthesis, evaluation, and opinion, then ask students to *discuss, reflect, evaluate, justify, advocate,* and *recommend.* Choosing and varying the verbs that you use to direct performance can guide students to the performance you wish to elicit. Enjoy the rest of the week.
Nelson

Enhancing Online Instruction No. 39: Intellectual Standards
[Research] [06/25/20]
Good morning, professors. Please accept this brief note drawn from a research study summarized in *A Guide to Online Course Design,* showing how to raise the typically low intellectual standard students share online.

As natural and ubiquitous as it has become, online communication has a low and imprecise inquiry level. Prompt students to raise that inquiry level to meet academic and professional standards in these areas:

1. *Clarity,* encouraging one another to elaborate further, illustrate meanings, and given examples;
2. *Accuracy,* encouraging one another to confirm, investigate, verify, and test critical assertions;
3. *Precision,* encouraging one another to be more specific, give details, and generally be exact;

4. *Relevance*, encouraging one another to relate statements to the issue, show bearing, and explain impact;
5. *Depth*, encouraging one another to articulate factors, examine complexities, and discern difficulties;
6. *Breadth*, encouraging one another to take an alternative perspective, consider others' views, and examine in other ways;
7. *Logic*, encouraging one another to make sense, fit one statement to another, and connect evidence to conclusion;
8. *Significance*, encouraging one another to articulate the import, identify central ideas, and prioritize importance; and
9. *Fairness*, encouraging one another to examine biases and correct to achieve equity.

Ensure that your online inquiries are raising the intellectual standard in these ways. Encourage students to question one another and their own assertions to meet higher inquiry standards. And enjoy the last of the week.
Nelson

Enhancing Online Instruction No. 40: Rubric Forms
[Research] [06/26/20]
Good morning, professors. Please accept this brief note about the different forms of rubric you may choose to adopt to assist your students in meeting performance expectations precisely. You know a rubric's power to guide learning. Do you, though, know its flexibility and sensitivity?

Generally, rubrics measure each significant aspect of performance from *non-performing*, to *basic but incompetent* performance, then *competent* performance and finally *mastery*. How, though, does one measure each stage? Many rubrics characterize non-performing simply as not doing critical actions. List the critical actions that the non-performer has omitted, and you've adequately shown the non-performer what to improve.

The basic/incompetent performance can be harder to describe but begins by lauding the partial performance while critiquing what's missing from performance that makes it only basic/incompetent. Distinguishing the positive partial from the incomplete negative is the key. Moving students

158

from basic/incompetent to competent is obviously critical to instruction, making this articulation key.

Describe competent performance by identifying what makes the performance complete. Try, then, to articulate what keeps the performance from being masterful. This distinction can be subtle, but if you cannot describe it, then it may not exist in sufficiently objective form for instruction to address. Describing masterful performance is generally easiest because it need not critique.

Review your rubric to see if it guides students precisely enough for them to distinguish incompetent from competent and masterful performances. If we cannot describe it, then it may not be appropriate as an instructional goal. Enjoy the weekend.
Nelson

Enhancing Online Instruction No. 41: Self-Directed Learning Stages
[Assessment] [06/29/20]
Good morning, professors. Please consider this brief summary of research from educational psychologist and online-curriculum designer Tina Stavredes's book *Effective Online Teaching*, advocating that we recognize the stages in self-directed learning that our online adult learners have reached, so that we serve all those learners.

Drawing on others' work, Dr. Stavredes summarizes models that suggest learners move from dependent, where they expect professors to direct their activities, to interested, where they expect professors to motivate, to involved, where they expect professors to facilitate, and finally to self-directed, where they expect professors simply to consult or guide.

A self-directed learner has skills related to learning, some prior subject knowledge, ability to set their own goals, confidence and motivation, time-management skills, and ability to self-evaluate. Dependent learners may have none of these attributes, while interested and involved learners will have more of these attributes.

As you design your online instruction, recognize your need to support learners at all stages. Don't assume knowledge or skills, but also recognize that some learners will have advanced knowledge and skills. With each unit and method, design for both appropriate learner support

159

but also appropriate learner independence. Foster self-directed learning while aiding those unable. And enjoy the last of the week.
Nelson

Enhancing Online Instruction No. 42: Scaffolding Strategies
[Research] [06/30/20]
Good morning, professors. Please accept this brief note drawn from *A Guide to Online Course Design* about the different forms of scaffolding strategies that a well-designed course follows. Scaffolding helps students link, navigate, and build, all necessary to efficient learning, these different ways:

procedural scaffolding ensures that students orient to your course with start-here information, your expectations, and a course roadmap;

metacognitive scaffolding ensures that students can plan (time estimates, checklists, organizers), monitor (discussion boards, study questions, flashcards, problems), and evaluate (model answers, explanations, rubrics, and feedback opportunities);

conceptual scaffolding ensures that students can build knowledge frameworks out of which to select, recall, and apply concepts. Here, students need worksheets (at all levels from vocabulary and outlines to problems and scenarios), templates, and knowledge maps;

strategic scaffolding ensures that students have access to you for just-in-time support, to identify resources, share alternative explanations, and demonstrate application.

Examine your online course to see if you are providing these different forms of scaffolding. And enjoy the week.
Nelson

Enhancing Online Instruction No. 43: Field-Dependent Learners
[Research] [07/01/20]
Good morning, professors. Please consider this brief note drawn from Dr. Stavredes's book *Effective Online Teaching*, on how to support field-dependent learners.

Study has shown that field-dependent learners mistake discrete new items within a subject as not discrete but instead dependent on the subject as a whole. Because they fail to disaggregate the new item from its context to learn its proper operation, they misunderstand items, confuse them with other concepts, and especially flounder when facing disorganized material with unclear learning goals.

To help field-dependent learners, provide organizers and scaffolds into which those learners can separate and place discrete new items. Much of law is logical in this way, such as claims or charges with elements, definitions, and exceptions, or rules with procedures and protocols. Then, design practice opportunities for students to spot, separate, place, and apply those items.

Studies show that field-independent learners perform more accurately, swiftly, and consistently, with greater internal motivation. Teach field independence, and you will have taught learning skills. Enjoy the week. Nelson

Enhancing Online Instruction No. 44: Choosing Technology
[Research] [07/02/20]
Good morning, professors. Please accept this brief note from organizational developers Palloff and Pratt's *Lessons from the Virtual Classroom* (summarizing another researcher's model) as to how to choose online technologies depending on your instructional objective:

1. Choose for *interaction* between professor and students, among students, or between students and course materials. Synchronous or asynchronous online communication including discussion boards, and course-management-system posted materials and links, form an interaction foundation;

2. Choose for *introspection* by students to interpret, revise, and apply concepts. Course-management-system programmed exercises, quizzes, journals, and assignments, and in-class exercises using polls, surveys, and problems, provide an introspection foundation;

3. Choose for *innovation* to address multiple learning needs and preferences, experimenting with audio and video, different assessment forms, and different access and feedback forms;

4. Choose for *integration* to draw together data, concepts, procedures, and theories, into applications, using case studies, simulations, role plays, and student-produced audio, video, and graphic presentations; and

5. Choose for *information* to ensure that students have the vocabulary, conceptual understanding, data, content, and context to achieve the learning goals. Readings and recorded or live lectures are traditional offerings, but consider online video with embedded quizzes, allowing peer-to-peer instruction, and using other higher-engagement means.

You are already doing these things, but sometimes seeing in a new or more-organized way what you are doing helps to reinforce best practices. Keep at it, and enjoy the weekend.
Nelson

Enhancing Online Instruction No. 45: Mobile Learning
[Research] [07/03/20]
Good morning, professors. Please accept this brief note, drawn in part from the book *Lessons from the Virtual Classroom*, about mobile learning. You may tend to think of an online course as focused on students using laptop or desktop-computer technology. Students, though, may have a greater capability to draw online instruction through their cell phones.

You've been there: stuck waiting somewhere, probably in a motor vehicle, aimlessly scrolling through news feeds and other cell-phone flotsam. Think of students: why not study instead? Those precious minutes quickly add up to hours. Why not help your students capture that otherwise-wasted time for studies?

Open your Canvas page in your cell-phone Canvas app. Examine your videos, outlines, quizzes, flashcards, and exercises. Are they cell-phone readable (optimized)? If not, then make them so. If so, then encourage students to capture those lost moments in studies. Doing so will also space their learning usefully.

To work my way through my undergraduate degree at a night school, I read my college course textbooks while exercising show horses on a treadmill. Talk about time capture. Give students a chance to time

162

manage smartly. Create, post, and advertise mobile-learning resources. And enjoy the week.
Nelson

Enhancing Online Instruction No. 46: Group Development Online
[Research] [07/06/20]
Good morning, professors. Please accept this brief note drawn from *Lessons from the Virtual Classroom* on how groups (classes) develop socially online, for best instruction.

Ideally, groups move from preforming to performing. How, though, do they do so? An instructor starts with *safety tasks* that ensure sound, organized, respectful, full participation. The instructor then moves the group toward *affinity tasks* that foster a sense of shared excitement over a subject and group endeavor larger than the participating individuals.

Next, the instructor moves the group through *dependence tasks* that require all students to participate equally, such as rotating case recitation and requiring completion of online exercises. Then, though, the instructor should move on to *independence tasks* that encourage differing thought, views, and reflections enlarging the group's scope and strengthening its character.

In a perfect class, the instructor moves on to *risk-taking tasks* that encourage civil disagreement, constructive criticism, and productive collaboration of students of differing skills and experiences. You've had such a class, perhaps many. With a little adaptation to online discussion boards, private chats, breakout rooms, and the like, you can have such classes online. Go for it. And enjoy the week.
Nelson

Enhancing Online Instruction No. 47: Reverse Engineering
[Research] [07/07/20]
Good morning, professors. Please accept this brief note drawn from two online instructional designer's book *A Guide to Online Course Design* encouraging that we reverse engineer our online courses for best design.

The online environment seems so different from the classroom that we may tend to focus on those differences, like mastering the technology, believing incorrectly that's what online instruction takes.

A better approach than making the medium the message, or the method, is to think first of what students must do. Then determine how to measure (assess) what students must do.

Only then should we plan instruction, then develop and implement instruction. Then remember to evaluate instruction against the goal that we first determined, using the assessment that we discerned. Reverse engineer your online course. And enjoy the week.
Nelson

Enhancing Online Instruction No. 48: Online Student Skills
[Research] [07/08/20]
Good morning, professors. Please accept this brief note from *A Guide to Online Course Design* on the technology skills students need to do well in online courses, drawn from a study of learner readiness. Students bring to online courses disparate technology-related skills. Students with stronger technology-related skills will perform better in online courses. Consider these skills:

1. *Computer literacy*, where students need to access the online course in the learning-management software, use word processing, spreadsheets, and visual media, participate in assessments, and troubleshoot technology issues;
2. *Information literacy*, where students need to access online libraries and databases using browsers and search software and terms, while evaluating the source, quality, breadth, and sufficiency of the information;
3. *Time management*, where students need to determine time necessary for online activities, prioritize those activities, and assess use of time to ensure timely completion of online modules and units;
4. *Communication*, where students need to be able to use email, messaging, social media, discussion boards, teleconference, and videoconference systems to project an online presence sharing information accurately and professionally.

Do not underestimate the differences among students as they develop and strengthen these critical online skills. Help students who may struggle with these skills, by modeling, coaching, referring for technical help, and offering alternative online activities and forums. Enjoy the weekend.
Nelson

Enhancing Online Instruction No. 49: Career Coaching
[Methods] [07/09/20]
Good morning, professors. Please accept this brief note on how to integrate career counseling into online instruction, to help students connect the discipline of present studies with the reward of future careers.

You've already seen how in a shared file like this one you can periodically invite students to share brief online reflections with one another on their professional experience, elevator speech of what to do with their degree, greatest possible achievement, first fun thing to do after success, and something they'll never do in a law career. These reflections can help students discern their commitments and identities.

Yet you can use the same shared file to help students identify specific steps, like networking through friends and family, joining a professional association, conducting an informational interview, that they can and perhaps should take to investigate and pursue those careers. These inquiries, posed once a class or every other class, can provide a career-relevant interlude to the intensity of your engaged online instruction.

These brief asides can also help students maintain social presence online, thus increasing their confidence, trust, and engagement. I hope you see something useful here. Enjoy the last of the week.
Nelson

Enhancing Online Instruction No. 50: Degree (Career) Value
[Morale] [07/10/20]
Good morning, professors. Please accept this brief note about the lurking question of the value of a degree earned in part online and the larger value of a career pursued after online instruction.

165

You've seen in a prior message that online researchers encourage us to correct the myth that a degree earned online has less value. To the contrary, well-designed online instruction can impart the same degree of rigor and hone the same or similar skills as those acquired in the classroom. Students who trust that to be the case may engage to a greater degree in online instruction and thus indeed learn more efficiently and effectively.

What, though, about the larger question of a career pursued based on an online degree? Law careers are somewhat unusual in that respect in that licensing, not the degree form or institution, is the career-access key. Your law school probably doesn't matter to the client if you have the knowledge, skills, and ethics, and can price and deliver your services responsibly. It surely doesn't matter to the opposing party or counsel and shouldn't matter to the judge.

In a sense, the current online environment is a great leveler. Competency is now all about performance rather than the instruction's location, history, tradition, or milieu. Prove students competent, and show them winning. Enjoy the weekend.
Nelson

Enhancing Online Instruction No. 51: Parable's Power
[Morale] [07/13/20]
Good morning, professors. Below for your mulling is an illustration of the power of parable, a tool that online instruction may also appropriately employ. Enjoy the week.
Nelson

He smirked at a colleague, rolling his eyes and raising his eyebrows, as the trainer walked in. His colleague smirked back. He'd almost skipped the training, like nearly all his colleagues. But he'd once been a reformer of his teaching, and something had called him not to skip this training, even though he wasn't happy being here.

The trainer began: "A ruler threw a banquet for his court, though few showed up. 'Where are my officials?' the ruler asked his adjutant, who answered that they'd been invited but had professed better things to be done. 'Then go into the hallways and commons, inviting anyone in,' the ruler replied, adding, 'The banquet is for all who wish to honor my rule.'"

Hearing this odd beginning, he turned in his seat toward his colleague. Just then, he noticed several teaching assistants, staffers, and adjuncts in the back of the classroom, whom he hadn't noticed or hadn't acknowledged when they came in. They were all smiling appreciatively at the odd parable, the meaning of which he wasn't quite ready to pursue.

Enhancing Online Instruction No. 52: Returning to Class
[Morale] [07/14/20]
Good morning, professors. Please accept the brief vignette below suggesting an important attitude when adjusting to the challenges of new online instruction. Enjoy the week.
Nelson

The professor paused as she prepared for the first class of the term. How long has she been teaching? That long?! The number didn't surprise her. She knew she'd been teaching law for a long time. What surprised her, what made the number seem wrong, was that she didn't think of herself as a senior professor, a fully formed instructor. No, she still thought of herself as a work in progress.

Indeed, she insisted on considering herself as unfinished, malleable, impressionable, adaptable, and exploring. She identified most strongly with her newest colleagues, those who of necessity were still exploring their new craft, and those among her more-experienced colleagues who shared her humility. She had to approach each term as if she had yet to discover something critical to the success of one or more of her new students.

She didn't like the alternative, which was that her usual practices, the things that she tended to do from term to term, might someday bind her. Yes, those practices had proven mostly sound. Those practices had helped many students. But she knew that as valuable as they might be they had also frustrated, distracted, and confused some students, those whom her instruction had not been able to reach in the past term. She had much to learn about learning.

Enhancing Online Instruction No. 53: Facing Uncertainty
[Morale] [07/15/20]
Good morning, professors. Please accept the brief vignette below suggesting an attitude toward meeting the challenges of the new online instruction. And enjoy the rest of the week.
Nelson

As Week 1 classes began, she couldn't help looking back over the uncertainty of the past few weeks stirred by, of all things, a virus. She wanted to see some humor in a virus crashing her world, when she would have predicted a half-dozen other things first to do so, whether terror attacks, nuclear war, melting ice caps, accreditation loss, identify theft, or getting hit by a truck. But humor, while somewhat relieving, didn't yet feel appropriate.

Instead, all that she found herself able to do was to dig in again, to begin again this term to care deeply for students, one by one, day by day, class by class, exam by exam. She turned again to learning the names of new students, beginning again to discover their histories, affinities, commitments, and ambitions.

In this toxic mix of social distancing, job losses, investment losses, and other profound disruption, teaching seemed to take on more, rather than less, meaning. Teaching meant normalcy, not to mention income and health insurance. But more than that, it meant hope, not primarily for her but for students. More than anything, she needed to see in their faces, to hear from their hearts, that they had hope for their futures. And she was now, once again, a part of their hope and their futures, a precious role indeed.

Enhancing Online Instruction No. 54: Integrating New and Old Forms
[Morale] [07/16/20]
Good morning, professors. Please accept this brief vignette suggesting how the online instruction we have pursued this term may enhance classroom instruction in the future. Enjoy the last of the week.
Nelson

The new online instruction late the prior term had gotten her thinking that she should incorporate some of its reforms into her classroom instruction. If some of what she had done online engaged students remotely, then maybe some of the same methods would engage students in class. Yes, the classroom environment itself was engaging, but, she'd learned, only in an alluring sort of way.

Studies had shown that in-class student demeanor--the smiling faces and nodding agreement--are deceiving. Students may be daydreaming at the same time that they mimic rapt attention. And the opposite is also true: students may be thinking productively, whether critically, evaluatively, or reflectively, when they instead appear to be daydreaming. She didn't know what students were really doing.

And so she decided to incorporate in class, her remote online forms that she had used to increase remote-student engagement. Instead of posing a question to the whole class, and either waiting for a volunteer or calling on someone, all students in class would answer the several electronically posed, summary questions, one by one, as she reached each point in the lecture, slideshow, and discussion. And she would immediately show the collective results to the class, just as she had done online. Now, that's enhancement, she concluded.

Enhancing Online Instruction No. 55: A Term's Worth of Work
[Morale] [07/17/20]
Good morning, professors. Please accept this brief vignette about the labor necessary to incorporate new methods and an attitude toward that labor that may help accomplish it. Enjoy the weekend.
Nelson

As she resolved to add a certain weekly enhancement to her courses, the realization settled in that she had a lot of work ahead of her. She had to replicate the enhancement for every week of each of her courses. If one week's enhancement for just one of her courses took her about an hour of concentrated time, then that meant that she had dozens of hours of instructional development ahead of her.

She'd been here before, many times facing what initially seemed like a mountain of work. At its outset, work of this kind always seemed daunting if not insurmountable, with everything else that she had to do.

169

She didn't have that kind of free time. Yet she knew at the same time that once she got started on it, learned the form, and refined the format, the work would probably take a lot less time than she had estimated.

More significantly, she knew that she needed this kind of deep background work, something productive on which to fall back when immediate tasks did not occupy her. She must be developing her skill and craft at all times, not simply treading water. She had to be growing, transforming, renewing. She had to be creative, productive, employed in a fresh and challenging way. She'd climbed these mountains before, and she relished the view from their peaks.

Enhancing Online Instruction No. 56: Learning's Subversive Nature
[Morale] [07/20/20]
Good morning, professors. Please accept this brief note about the subversive nature of true learning, deep learning, the kind that connects experiences and commitments with new opportunities based on new knowledge and skills. And enjoy the week.
Nelson

Wow, she thought, as she watched the new students file into the classroom for the term's start: **they have no idea what's coming.**

She had realized only that morning, while reflecting yet again on learning's mysterious nature, just how subversive learning is. No, not in the political or ideological sense. She didn't want to change student values, identities, affinities, ambitions, and commitments. Just the opposite was true: she hoped that students preserved those things that had brought them here. Learning wasn't about adopting a professor's politics, not even about accepting a professor's authority or view.

Learning isn't indoctrination, which is simply conformity in any case, not at all subversive. She didn't want students merely to find a new conformity. Learning is instead subversive because it requires students to reorganize fixed patterns of thought. If all students did was to attach her information to their prior patterns of thought, then she would have failed. If instead they retained their values and commitments but deployed them through new and more-powerful patterns, more-logical, reasoned, and persuasive new forms, then students would have succeeded in its subversive goal.

170

Enhancing Online Instruction No. 57: Indirect Instruction
[Methods] [07/21/20]
Good morning, professors. Please accept this brief vignette suggesting the power of indirect instruction to correct fixed mindsets that interfere with learning. Enjoy the week.
Nelson

Now this construct was new, she thought. She had heard from a colleague that morning about the power, indeed at times the necessity, of an indirect approach to learning. She hadn't at first understood what her colleague had meant. But then it clicked.

Direct instruction in the concepts that students needed to learn was fine, indeed wholly necessary. But at times, direct instruction only hardened students against what they needed to learn. No matter how many times she told students, drilled students, and had students rehearse, some concepts some students just refused to learn. Their existing mental construct was impervious to direct confrontation.

Instruction had instead to first undermine the impervious construct, disrupt it, not by battering it but by inviting it, piquing its curiosity, subtly undermining it. How? Parable. Allegory. Metaphor. Something that caused the student's impervious state to awake, let down its defenses, and seek. Now, this revelation she needed to explore and deploy.

Enhancing Online Instruction No. 58: Pleasure in the Quotidian
[Morale] [07/22/20]
Good morning, professors. Online instruction takes additional detailed steps that the instructor must execute timely and correctly, at risk of disrupting instruction. Please accept this brief vignette suggesting how to approach repetitive but important or critical tasks, completing them with the accuracy and timeliness that they demand. Enjoy the rest of the week.
Nelson

As Week 2 of the term got into full swing, and the impact of supporting the learning, ambitions, and emotions of her many new students simultaneously settled somewhat heavily in, she realized the comfort that

171

she took in her job's small things. She'd had other jobs before becoming a law professor, and not all of them had such small pleasures. Timekeeping as a lawyer and, before that, busing tables as a server and cleaning kennels as a youth, were not what she thought of as pleasures.

But a law professor? Preparing a syllabus, writing and rearranging exams, reorganizing a course-management page, yet again? She could see these repetitive tasks as annoying, distracting, cumbersome--but she didn't. Mundane, yes. Quotidian, yes. But they were clean, accessible, clear, concise, and oddly satisfying in their order. Maybe she was just satisfying her obsessive-compulsive nature, but it didn't matter. She liked these small things lifting her past the sometimes-fearsome burden of holding up student expectations, ensuring that students were learning, and ensuring that she was treating students fairly, rigorously, equitably, and as they deserved.

Enhancing Online Instruction No. 59: Staying Organized
[Methods] [07/23/20]
Good morning, professors. Please accept this brief note suggesting one method for keeping your online courses organized. Online courses involve constantly sharing resources, exercises, and activities online. How do you keep all your online files readily available that term *and repeatable for the following term*?

Your Google Drive offers you Docs (word processing), Sheets (spreadsheets), and Forms (surveys) through which to engage students in class. You may, like me, be sharing two, three, four, or more such files with students every week in each of your online courses, while you also have files that you use across several or all weeks.

Consider creating in your Google Drive one folder for each of your courses, giving it the course name (e.g., Property I, Lansing Section). Within each course folder, store the files that you share across several or all weeks, in my case Careers, Rewards, and Assessment Corrections files. Also store here administrative files, in my case Emails, Messages (repeated, to copy and paste), and Prayer (yes, I pray for specific students).

Then, within each course folder, create a Weekly Files subfolder. In that subfolder, make folders for Week 1, Week 2, etc., through term's end. In each of those weekly files, store the two, three, four, or more files that you share for just that week. These weekly subfolders help you quickly navigate to all files for each week, while stepping up to the course folder lets you quickly navigate to general files that you use across several weeks. Next term, you can follow the same week-to-week order.

I hope this note gives you some encouragement for staying organized online. A folder system for your course and each week of your course, whether in Google Drive or another location, can make order out of chaos while saving time. Enjoy the rest of the week.
Nelson

Enhancing Online Instruction No. 60: Student Interaction
[Methods] [07/24/20]
Good morning, professors. Please accept this brief note about the need to supply substantial interaction in online courses.

The journal *Inside Higher Ed* recently ran an opinion piece arguing that despite the pandemic-induced paradigm shift away from the classroom, online learning will never replace the classroom because students routinely report that they hate it.

The opinion repeats common criticisms, like the distractibility, lack of accountability, and lack of structure of the online environment, especially in asynchronous courses. But students' major criticism had to do with the lack of spontaneous interaction so characteristic of the classroom.

The opinion, though, admits that online courses can offer student/professor and student/student interaction. We engage students interactively in well-conducted videoconference sessions (both orally and using the chat function) and well-designed breakout sessions, and using discussion boards and even email.

Know that students value interaction highly and that rigorous interaction can promote the deep processing that aids learning. Design for interaction. Create and sustain a dynamic online environment. And enjoy the weekend.
Nelson

Enhancing Online Instruction No. 61: Identity Affirmation
[Methods] [07/27/20]
Good morning, professors. Please accept this brief note suggesting ways in which to affirm student identity in the online learning environment, as those who have long studied online learning recommend.

The authors of this *Inside Higher Ed* opinion piece argue after decades of study that affirming student identity is critical to student engagement and performance in the online learning environment. The classroom does so, naturally. You know how well you come to know students in the classroom. The question is, can you reproduce that level of familiarity, suggesting student identity affirmation, in your online courses?

Early in the term, ask students to share with you and one another, career-relevant information about themselves, as in this Careers file and Rewards file. Then, when engaging students orally in your videoconference class, around case recitation, problem work, or other online activities, look for opportunities to recognize their individual identity, drawing on your knowledge of their experience, interests, and ambitions.

We can help students share and affirm their identity online. You'll know when you've done so: when you and students share a familiarity with one another and affinity for one another that feels like the classroom. Enjoy the week.
Nelson

Enhancing Online Instruction No. 62: AWOL Students
[Methods] [07/28/20]
Good morning, professors. Please accept this brief note about how to treat students who disappear from your online course, in the vernacular, going AWOL (away without leave). Catching up with withdrawn students in an in-person class can be easier because of their physical presence. In online courses, students disappear more easily.

Students check out and disappear from online courses in various ways including joining the class by audio only, repeatedly joining and dropping out of the class, not responding to audio inquiries in class, not participating in online exercises, not completing required exercises, and even missing exams or submitting incomplete assignments or exams.

First, don't ignore students who disappear online. Reach out to them, not in class in front of other students in a way that could embarrass them, but by email, videoconference, or telephone. Persist, even when they don't persist, but do so respectfully, out of concern.

If they don't respond or they respond vaguely, and remain unaccountable to your online class despite your persistent intervention, alert your campus assistant dean who may know more about the student's situation and be able to help you re-engage the student.

If you find more than the rare student withdrawing, disengaging, and disappearing, then consider modifying your instructional approach. Some study suggests that more student-centered rather than instructor-centered designs, and flexible designs that give students choices for how to participate, may reduce attrition.

Above all, keep your faith in student commitment. Exhibit belief that the disappearing student can persist. Students who make dramatic academic recoveries report that the belief of just one professor in their capability and commitment made a critical difference. Enjoy the week.
Nelson

Enhancing Online Instruction No. 63: Topic Videos
[Methods] [07/29/20]
Good morning, professors. Please accept this brief note about using relevant video in your online course to enhance engagement. One of the advantages to an online course is that you are already in the virtual environment, where using video to enhance design is natural, seamless.

Creating your own videos is one option, for flipped lectures, worked problems, example essay scoring, and skills demonstrations, among other methods. Letting students create and share instructional videos, worked problems, and demonstrations is another sound option.

Yet you can also quickly enhance topic lectures and presentations using compelling video available on the internet. Here, for example, are faked motor-vehicle accidents (insurance fraud), genuine car crashes, car-crash animations made for lawyers, and workplace accidents, that I use before class and during class breaks, to illustrate Torts II Week 11 no-fault and worker's comp studies.

You can also readily find lawyer-skills videos online for things like taking depositions, motion practice, direct and cross-examination, and other litigation skills. You can also find video examples of lawyer misconduct, in depositions for instance.

You don't need to take precious class time to show relevant video but can let video run during down times before and after class, and on class breaks. Explore videos that can illustrate your topics while engaging students with compelling examples. And enjoy the rest of the week.
Nelson

Enhancing Online Instruction No. 64: Law Details
[Methods] [07/30/20]
Good morning, professors. Please accept this brief note about how to help students learn, recall, and apply more detail within the law frameworks that you introduce.

We've all had the experience of evaluating student work where the bulk of students comprehend, recall, and apply the basic law framework, perhaps the elements of a claim or charge, or the conditions for a constitutional or procedural test. They think and write like students learning a new topic.

Yet then, one or two students, or a handful of students, display the remarkable ability to recall and apply law details, nuances that as field experts we know make the critical difference in genuine cases. How, we've all thought, do those few students exhibit such mastery? They should go straight to graduation.

My usual thought is, well, they came from a family of lawyers, or they grew up arguing at the dinner table, or tiger mom home schooled them from the crib. But attributing learning to innate qualities, prior learning, or advanced skill are only crutches, lost opportunities, and a rejection of our role. We should instead think: how can I help more students master law details?

The answer may be in building clearer, more-articulated scaffolds into our basic law frameworks. We succeed in helping students learn the frameworks. Maybe we just need to articulate those frameworks with greater detail, ensuring that students have the links and scaffolds to learn and recall those details, and the practice to apply them.

For some years, while I work out, I've been listening to podcasts of Bible scholars discussing both their topics and their instruction, from which this intentional scaffolding has become ever clearer to me. Every main point has chains of hyperlinks to subsidiary points that the topic invites students to learn. Our role should be to highlight, scaffold, articulate those hyperlinks. Enjoy the last of the week.
Nelson

Enhancing Online Instruction No. 65: Vygotsky Scaffolding
[Methods] [07/31/20]
Good morning, professors. Please accept this brief note, suggested by yesterday's message, about how to use scaffolding to increase student learning.

Scaffolding is one of those awkward, wonky instructional terms that law professors prefer to avoid. What it intends to imply is that students learn most and best when bridging from their current knowledge and skill toward things that they do not yet know and cannot yet do. The scaffold helps them reach the heights of new learning.

A key to effective scaffolding is to get students working in their zone of proximal development--another wonky phrase. Obviously, we want students to develop. But scaffolding suggests that to do so, they must work *near, but not within*, what they already know and can do--proximal, not remote. Too-advanced work, and the student learns nothing. Too-near work, and the student learns little.

Thus, what we need to do as instructors is to link what students know with what they barely don't know, and then get them working in those proximal don't-know areas with others who do know and can guide them to knowing. Find a fuller description here. Oh, and Vygotsky? A fascinating Russian psychologist who pioneered rich concepts of learning. Try his *Thought and Language*. And enjoy the weekend.
Nelson

Enhancing Online Instruction No. 66: Scaffolding Tips
[Methods] [08/03/20]
Good morning, professors. Please accept this brief note sharing four tips, drawn from the summary shared in the last message, on how to improve your instructional scaffolds, those bridges that help students get from what they know and do to reach what they don't know and can't do.

First, know what students know and don't know, and can do and can't do. You may be assuming knowledge students don't yet have or, equally fruitless, already have. Be ready to adjust your instruction to that ideal near-what-they-know zone. And be ready to offer a range of zones to accommodate both advanced and beginning students.

Second, encourage students to interact with you and other students who have different knowledge and skill levels. Learning speeds when guided by others who have advanced knowledge and skills, and challenged by others who have less knowledge and skill. If mixed-level group work is difficult online, then offer mixed-level exercises where students can practice basic, intermediate, and advanced skills.

Third, while guiding student learning, don't offer too much guidance. Let students struggle and explore some. Give them guiding questions and instructions more so than direct answers. Fourth, and relatedly, have students think aloud or write out their thought process. Help students reveal and evaluate their thinking, in a metacognitive manner where they can adjust their approach. And while you're at it, explain your own thought process.

These instructional activities may not sound much like law school, but they are fundamental to learning. Keep pursuing learning. And enjoy the week.
Nelson

Enhancing Online Instruction No. 67: Instruction as Art
[Reflection] [08/04/20]
Good morning, professors. As we near the end of another term, please accept this brief encouragement about how a course becomes like a work of art after we complete it.

178

Analogies can be both misleading and revealing, unhelpful or inspirational. Instruction is surely more science than art. Rigorous method, measurement, assessment, and adjustment are important tools in instruction's logic and science. Instruction has outcomes, critical to students and important to the institution, although more remote to the instructor.

Yet one can look back on a completed course, seeing it more like art than science. Creating a masterwork of art typically requires deep conception, a profound understanding of the subject that reveals things others do not see, creating in the artist a desire to share the revelation. Masterworks also require design, thoughtful structure for the coming piece.

Masterworks also require knowledge of the medium, the properties of the substances and procedures the artist will choose and use. Masterworks also require sound knowledge and acute study of light and perspective. In their execution, masterworks also require layering, building up of the work from foundation to final flourish.

Look back across the term, appreciating the art with which you pursued student learning in your course. What do you see? Now look forward to the next term. What do you need to see? Enjoy the week.
Nelson

Enhancing Online Instruction No. 68: Reflection as Profession
[Reflection] [08/05/20]
Good morning, professors. Please accept this brief note, here in the last week of instruction during the term, on the value of reflection on one's profession. During the term, we may have little time for processing what is happening in our courses. Review and exam weeks, and breaks, lend time for reflection.

A traditional form of reflection has to do with evaluating your own strengths and weaknesses, while identifying opportunities you can pursue within your reach and risks you can minimize. Another professional form has us evaluate how well we are fulfilling responsibilities, what external factors are influencing our work, what we most desire to pursue, what leadership opportunities we have, and what we hope to achieve.

Reflective teaching practice, though, can take on a deeper, more-transformative goal of identifying, questioning, and confirming or modifying one's beliefs about potential for learning and how one learns. What deepens one's expertise is often not one's sense of one's own self, things like strengths, interest, and goals, but of the subject (in this instance learning) itself. How we think about teaching and learning becomes what we expect students to do, and what we get students doing becomes how they learn.

Take review and exam week, and the break, to reflect over your assumptions about learning. Can we even articulate how we believe students learn? And how does what we articulate align with what empirical evidence shows? Reflect on your profession. You earned it. Enjoy the rest of the week.
Nelson

Enhancing Online Instruction No. 69: Reducing Isolation
[Methods] [08/06/20]
Good morning, professors. Please accept this brief note sharing a method for reducing the harmful isolation that remote students can feel when studying online.

Survey the research on the effect of isolation on learning, and you will find evidence of negative effects on students, instructors, and parents or other supporters of students. The isolation natural to remote learning has generally negative effects.

One researcher suggests in this article that we can reduce that negative effect, and reduce the remote student's sense of isolation, by offering three-to-five minute podcasts from other students describing ways to improve studies.

Late in this term, I asked students to create those podcasts for new students next term. Here are my brief instructions to students and the folder of podcasts that I received, reviewed, and approved for offer next term. Consider giving it a try. And enjoy the last of the week.
Nelson

Enhancing Online Instruction No. 70: Introducing Clients
[Methods] [08/07/20]
Good morning, professors. Please accept this brief note showing a method to help students think about clients whom they'd like to serve in your subject's field. Helping clients connect your course's topics with law-practice opportunities can increase their engagement. Here's one way to do so.

Create a Google Form (survey) like this one. Think of the half-dozen or so most-compelling, least-compelling, and typical clients you might encounter in your field. For each client, ask the student to rank their interest in serving that client, from strong interest to zero interest.

At the form's end, you can also have students list the same half-dozen or so clients in order of priority, from those they'd most like to represent to least like to represent, as in this form. You might also end the form by inviting the student to describe their ideal client.

Lawyers don't always get to choose their clients, but lawyers do know who their clients tend to be, who they'd like to represent, and who'd they'd prefer not to represent. Help students think about those opportunities. And enjoy the break.
Nelson

Enhancing Online Instruction No. 71: Illustrating Memory
[Methods] [09/07/20]
Good morning, professors, and I hope you enjoyed the break. Please accept this brief note about illustrating for students how they can help themselves remember what they learn.

As instructors, we know well the model that learners briefly hold presented new information in working memory, move it to short-term memory when processing (elaborating, using) the information, and move it to long-term memory when repeating (spacing and interleaving) the information.

This simple model should compel students to practice these methods (elaborate to move to short term, repeat at intervals to move to long term). How, though, can we illustrate this model for students and periodically remind them of it? Attached is a slide illustration that you

may adopt, adapt, and periodically drop into your weekly instruction. Enjoy the week.
Nelson

Enhancing Online Instruction No. 72: Verbal De-Escalation
[Morale] [09/08/20]
Good morning, professors. Law school stresses students, especially under circumstances like the present one necessitating online instruction. Please accept these tips, drawn from an employee mental-health service, on how to de-escalate anger from students suffering high stress:

- *preserve the student's dignity,* such as by moving the student to a private chat, even when the student does not act dignified;
- *acknowledge the anger and its impact* on the student rather than ignoring or minimizing it, or blaming the student;
- *listen actively and respectfully,* reflecting back what the student says but in more-neutral terms that defuse the anger;
- *don't take the anger personally* even when expressed personally because stress is the cause, not you, who are just the anger's target;
- *question respectfully, not inquisitorially,* to help the student identify the anger's source in the high stress;
- *remain calm but with intense focus* on the student, not treating the student offhandedly but helping the student regain composure;
- *align with a healthy part* of the student's expression, whatever you find that shows the student expressing a calmer way forward; and
- *problem-solve together*, while accepting responsibility for any part you played in causing the student's stress.

I hope you find these tips helpful in supporting the mental health of students during this continuing crisis requiring online instruction. Enjoy the rest of the week.
Nelson

Enhancing Online Instruction No. 73: Preparing for Online Class
[Methods] [09/09/20]
Good morning, professors. Please accept this brief note reminding us of how deep our preparation must be each week to seamlessly conduct an

engaging online class. Here are typical steps in which you might engage over the course of the week preparing for each class:

1. *develop the in-class assessment form*, or select from already-developed forms, you will use to help students determine their understanding;
2. *develop the engagement forms*, or select from already-developed forms, students will use for application exercises in class;
3. *develop the slideshow* or discussion notes, or adjust previously prepared slide show or notes, that you will use to introduce, organize, and pace the class;
4. *key assessment and engagement forms to your slideshow* or discussion notes so you know when to toggle to those exercises in class;
5. *schedule an email with links to the engagement forms*, to send to students at the start of class reminding them of file access;
6. *send students a reminder* of class with the Webex-meeting class link and class agenda, early in the day of class, to ensure access and preparation;
7. *review the previous week's class* for any follow-up matters students may have requested or you may have promised; and
8. *start the Webex meeting* at least a half hour before class for students to join to test connections.

These steps are the kind of detail-oriented, organized, structured activities that make for seamless online classes from week to week, without delays that interrupt instruction. You know when you've achieved it. Keep at it, and enjoy the last of the week.
Nelson

Enhancing Online Instruction No. 74: Statement Types
[Methods] [09/10/20]
Good morning, professors. Please accept this brief note suggesting that some students may need basic help differentiating forms of statements.

A recent survey that I made of Lansing and Grand Rapids sections shows that although it may be obvious to us that sentences can take the following different forms, those differences are not necessarily obvious to untrained students:

- *rules* define conditions governing conduct;

- *commands* dictate conduct;
- *prohibitions* prohibit conduct;
- *hypotheses* suggest possibilities to consider;
- *conclusions* assert reasoned judgments;
- *data* shares observations or information; and
- *questions* raise issues to address and answer.

We may assume student capacity to craft articulate analyses, when some students lack basic appreciation for different sentence forms. Be clear in the forms of sentences that you use and in your expectations for how students use them. Enjoy the last of the week.
Nelson

Conclusion

Teaching is a highly personal pursuit, even though its object (student learning) is entirely outside of oneself. Teaching, especially *professing* (being a professor of any kind but more so a *law* professor), demands identity. Students expect professors to be personalities. Professors readily oblige, the personality serving alternately as a tool for instruction and a crutch for instruction's failure. Once one assumes a workable identity, getting over the initial fear and incompetence, modifying or giving up that identity can be quite hard. Advice on teaching feels too personal, like a character attack, when the advice instead has an outside aim in enhancing student learning.

These messages, collected into a journal, don't so much as reflect a sensitivity toward professor identity as *overwhelm* identity. One sees from the above professor's daily journal that *so much* goes on around learning that any professor's personality, preferences, maybe a few foibles and eccentricities, are pretty much irrelevant. Professors can be charming at times, irascible at other times. We can be extraordinarily committed at times, seemingly indifferent at other times. What matters, as in so many other things, is the accumulation of our skill and effort, not the packages in which we present them.

The above messages should also have communicated how extraordinarily fluid teaching and learning are, and how privileged of an intellectual environment teaching and learning offer. Law professors and students do not worry very much about their physical security, even their physical fitness or simple hunger. Others meet their basic needs. Instead, they get to shoot for the moon, embark on that preposterous object of learning how to recall and use vast quantities of law to make the world better, or if not better, then survivable. What a noble goal law professors and students share. And what passion law professors show in pursuing it.

Acknowledgments

Please allow me to acknowledgment Western Michigan University Thomas M. Cooley Law School, its President and Dean James McGrath, and the law school's faculty members, staff, and students for sustaining a rigorous and vital spirit of investigation and excellence in teaching and learning. The above messages detail some of the many contributions of President McGrath and other individual faculty members who continue to light the flame for enhancing the skills of an already-skilled professoriate. One finds great privilege, and even greater grace, at every turn, and not just from faculty colleagues and supportive staff but especially from students. May wisdom continue to reveal more of her treasures.

CPSIA information can be obtained
at www.ICGtesting.com
Printed in the USA
FSHW010829250820
73187FS